By the Water of Girvan

The Valley first appeared in *Scottish Country* in 1938.

The Kilkerran Improvers is reprinted from *Lowland Lairds* (Faber and Faber 1949, reprinted 2003 by The Grimsay Press).

The Queen in Ayrshire, The Last Monks of Crossraguel, Master Robert Cathcart of Pinmore and the Carrick Feud, and **The Fortunes of William Niven,** are reprinted from *The White Hind* (Faber and Faber 1963, reprinted 2004 by The Grimsay Press).

The Weird of Drummochreen, Simple Annals, and **The Plague in Ayr - 1606** are reprinted from *The Man behind Macbeth* (Faber and Faber 1949, reprinted 2004 by The Grimsay Press).

A Wine-Merchant's Letter-Book is reprinted from *Essays Presented to Sir Lewis Namier* (ed by Richard Parsen, and A J P Taylor, Macmillan, 1956).

The Carriage with Yellow Wheels first appeared in *The Glasgow Herald* on 27 August, 1955

Dailly Church first appeared in *A Guide to Dailly Church.*

The Covenanter is previously unpublished.

By the Water of Girvan

People and places in
South Ayrshire history

Sir James Fergusson

Glasgow

The Grimsay Press

The Grimsay Press
an imprint of
Zeticula
57 St Vincent Crescent
Glasgow
G3 8NQ

http://www.thegrimsaypress.co.uk
admin@thegrimsaypress.co.uk

Photographs © Stuart Johnston 2005,
except page 188 (Brougham) by © Douglas Scott, 2005

First published in this form in Great Britain 2005

This is an expanded version of a
Private Limited Edition of Fifty copies, printed in May 2004

ISBN 1 84530 005 x Paperback
ISBN 1 84530 018 1 Hardback

Contents

List of Illustrations

Foreword

My father, who wrote these essays, used to maintain that for anyone lucky enough to live in the Girvan valley the only joy of travel must be the pleasure of coming home. That deep affection, made so plain in the first piece, written in 1938, was no doubt magnified by five years' absence during the war, and later by his twenty years as Keeper of the Records of Scotland, when he necessarily spent four days and nights of most weeks in Edinburgh. But the Register House gave him new opportunities for the exploration and writing which won him renown and respect as a scholar and historian; and the history of Scotland, of Ayrshire and of Kilkerran in particular, where his family papers were a uniquely rich primary source for research, never ceased to be his love and inspiration.

Between 1937 and 1972 he published fifteen books. Before the war, there were *The Letters of George Dempster to Sir Adam Fergusson* and the histories of *William Wallace, Guardian of Scotland* and *Alexander the Third.* After it came the story of *Argyll in the Forty-Five;* a valedictory account of the *Sixteen Peers of Scotland* - he conducted the last of their elections to the House of Lords that began with the Union and ended with the Act of 1963 ; and a filial examination of *The Curragh Incident,* in which the actions of his father, General Sir Charles Fergusson, were material in averting mutiny in the British Army on the eve of the First World War.

His last works included *The Man Behind Macbeth*, a persuasive discovery of a sixteenth-century model for Shakespeare's villain; and a biography of *Balloon Tytler,* Scotland's - and Britain's - first aeronaut.

He was meticulous in his approach to history. Proud of Scottish tradition when it was authentic, he once reflected on 'how much dearer to the popular mind in Scotland is the preservation of legend than the desire for historical truth'. Thus, following the example of his ancestor Lord Hailes in the 1770s, he rigorously questioned the myths that have sometimes driven and seduced Scotland's culture and politics - whether surrounding William Wallace or Robert Burns, the Forty-Five or the Appin murder. He demonstrated in *The Declaration of Arbroath* that that much-quoted letter to the Pope was intended to meet no more than the pressing needs of the 1320s hour; and elsewhere that the passage of the Act of Union through the Scottish Parliament neither distorted national feeling nor was obtained by bribery. It was in this vein that he publicly damned with the label 'plastic Scots' the post-war outbreak of Scottish poetry in a literary vernacular, 'lallans,' which nobody had ever spoken. He had as little time for pretension as for claptrap.

Next to history he loved literature. Among his close friends my father numbered such historians as Henrietta Tayler, Annie Dunlop, Lewis Namier and John Wheeler-Bennet; but he was no less close to Eric Linklater, Frederick Pottle, Wyndham Ketton-Cremer and Dover Wilson - the last, with a fine scorn for the opinions of A.L.Rowse in Oxford, was one of the few scholars who could teach him something new about Shakespeare. Shakespeare, Burns, Boswell, Austen, Scott: he wrote, or gave talks, about them all.

In his last years - he died in 1973 aged 69 - he set himself the task of reading the Waverley novels from start to finish (a few for the first time), and concluded that far too many were 'not really very good' and those that were little read deserved to remain so. He loved music, opera, the theatre, painting and architecture. His memory for the esoteric and the recondite was prodigious: which was why for many years, with the journalist Jack House, he represented Scotland in the radio programme *Round Britain Quiz*. Each was expert in broad but very different fields: my father knew who the Wizard of the North was (the same Walter Scott) but admiringly left it to his colleague to identify the Wizard of Dribble (Stanley Matthews); and they were never beaten. The sport he most enjoyed, as a member of the Queen's Body Guard for Scotland, was archery. Yet for exercise he was keenest on walking, in the Highlands when he was younger, closer to home later. He examined on foot all the places he wrote about, from Orkney to Whithorn, especially the battlefields, declaring that 'an historian's work cannot be done only in the study.'

***

The present anthology, culled from his other published collections, brings together those essays which deal more or less directly with the Girvan valley - the parts of it, at any rate, which demanded an historian's attention or awoke his curiosity. It is in no sense a full story of the valley: the principal estates lying on or near the river, like their people, make their appearance simply as the narratives dictate - Trochrague, Penkill, Killochan, Bargany, Dalquharran, Kilkerran, Kirkbride, Blairquhan.

The opening chapter flows naturally into the second, which is both an account of the establishment at Kilkerran in Georgian times of a Lowland agricultural and silvicultural estate and a family history. The business of 'improving' made this part of the valley what it is - although the exigencies of modern estate management have meant the dilapidation or disappearance of some miles of the eighteenth-century amenity paths through the woods and glens which were once kept clear and in repair by estate labour (for want of whom for some fifteen autumns my father used defiantly to rake up and burn the leaves himself).

Here, in a convincing identification of the author of the *Historie of the Kennedyis*, is a new angle on the Carrick feud which raged up, down and around the Water of Girvan in the reign of James VI; an account of how the young Mary Queen of Scots passed through Ayrshire in August 1563, crossing the river near its mouth; the weird (or fate) of a waterside farm which is now a heap of stones; and a sketch of a boyhood friend of Burns, a Maybole merchant who for four decades lived in Kirkbride, the next estate upstream from Kilkerran.

These pages include three of what Dr Johnson would have called 'fugitive pieces' which are surely too interesting to be lost. One is the guide written for Dailly Parish Kirk. This useful record is expanded in the accompanying chapter 'Simple Annals' which takes a closer look at Dailly's graves and the ancient inscriptions which were disappearing from them almost as my father copied them down. He was for many years an elder, and walked the two-and-a-half miles there every Sunday morning, habitually following the New Testament readings in the original Greek.

The second piece, written for the *Glasgow Herald*, features the black brougham with yellow wheels, red lines and a family crest on each door, in which his grandfather would ride to the Sunday services. It is now in the Glasgow Museum of Transport).

The other fugitive is the piece on an Ayrshire wine-merchant's letter-book, which originally appeared in a set of essays presented in 1956 to Sir Lewis Namier. This, like the study of the plague in Ayr, deserves its tenuous place in a book about the valley if only because, to all who lived nearby, wine shipped into the port of Ayr was of as critical interest as the pestilence - at a time when whisky was seldom drunk outside the Highlands and smugglers supplied brandy at overwhelmingly competitive prices.

The short poem at the end, inspired by the rediscovery of the covenanter's grave described in the first chapter, is patently the product of a sensitive and romantic mind - of a man, indeed, who was devoted no less to his living family than to honouring his forebears.

Adam Fergusson
2004

1

The Valley

The valley of which I have to tell lies in about the middle of Carrick, one of the three bailliaries into which the shire of Ayr was anciently divided. It forms a basin about five miles long and two wide from hill-crest to hill-crest; and through the middle of it flows a small river. Further north the river wanders aimlessly, until it bends back into the hills to the east from which it draws, through countless little leaping brown burns, the waters which feed it. But here it runs fairly straight, between calm green meadows where cattle graze, and stately woods of oak, beech, and fir. Its course is roughly from north-east to south-west, and when it passes out of the valley it has only a short distance to flow to reach the sea, or rather the lower part of the Firth of Clyde.

On the south-eastern side the hills rise to grassy moor and go tumbling away for barren miles towards the mountains of central Galloway. On the north-western there runs a long, wooded ridge from the top of which a magnificent view can be had of Arran, Kintyre, and Bute, with Ailsa Craig, that monstrous lump of an island, to the south, and the Argyll mountains to the north. This hill contains a vein of coarse coal and is noted for a legend, which can be traced back beyond the beginning of the eighteenth century, that it is on fire inside.

In any long-civilized country a landscape is like a very old parchment on which successive generations have written a record of their doings. The pumice-stone of time erases each record with varying thoroughness, but the palimpsest always retains something of the original inscription for observant eyes to read. The earliest records may be so faint that only the most skilful archaeologist can decipher them; but for the more recent ones quite a small knowledge of the district's history may make its traces astonishingly clear. The more you read or hear of occurrences which have taken place in a country familiar to you, the more plainly the marks of them stand out upon its face. It does not take long to realize that a landscape is history; that layer upon layer of its past lives on in its present; that each generation that inhabits the ground enjoys a part of the fruit of its predecessors' labours while it contributes something to the convenience, the comfort, or the pleasure of its successors.

Now the history of this valley and its inhabitants has been for a long time one of my favourite studies; and it is extraordinary how, the more I examine it, the more clearly certain of the earlier inscriptions on the palimpsest stands out, and the more superficial appear those of the last hundred and fifty years or so. The twentieth century has added almost nothing to the record; for the rebuilding of small houses or farm-buildings, or the cutting and re-planting of woods, produces no more than slight and temporary changes in the landscape as a whole. The nineteenth century added only a little: the railway, almost unnoticeable among the deep woods which conceal its passage along the north-western slope of the valley, two or three coal-pits equally well hidden, an extra stone bridge over the river, an enlargement of the area planted with trees, and an extension of hedges and fences. Generally speaking, it did no more than deepen the impressions of the eighteenth century, since which period the character of the valley, then chiefly created, has remained almost entirely unchanged. One important alteration, however, was made in the early part of the nineteenth century - the straightening and embanking of a part of the river's channel, to minimize flooding. This work was done in George IV's time, and it has made parts of the river a good deal less picturesque than, according to a pen-and-wash drawing of 1813, they used to be, though much less damaging to the surrounding pastures. Nowadays, after a few hours' heavy rain, a kind of reminiscence of the river's old course appears in the pools which fill the depressions in the fields where it used to run.

To start, however, with the earliest 'layer' of history's records of the valley, you must come up one of the glens cutting into its south-eastern side. Here stands a fragment of an ancient peel-tower. Seventy years ago it, was still nearly a complete building; but to-day there only remains one end-wall, entire from foundation to gable, showing the height of the original structure, and a heap of tumbled masonry, blurred by grass and bracken into a rough green mound. The age of this tower is beyond conjecture. It is supposed to be one of the oldest of its kind in Scotland to be built of hewn stone, and possibly dates back to the middle of the fourteenth century. But immeasurably older as a dwelling-place is a site about half a mile further up the glen, by the side of a burn tributary to that which splashes among the rocks below the tower. This is an oval-shaped mound standing in the hollow between two spurs of the hill sloping down to the burn. It is much shorter and narrower at the top than at the bottom; in other words, its sides slope steeply upwards to a flat top, which is about thirty yards long and ten or twelve wide.

The merest glance at this oddly shaped mound will tell you that it is not a natural structure. Its regularity is too striking to be accidental. Round its foot, moreover, runs a double bank, somewhat broken away here and there by the tunnelling of rabbits, but irresistibly suggesting an old rampart. The whole aspect of the place stamps it as not only an artificial construction, but a place of refuge and defence. It is known locally as 'the Moat Knowe,' and such amateur archaeologists as have seen it - I do not think an expert has ever been here - have agreed in calling it a 'pre-historic' stronghold. It is a vague but obvious conclusion: no more can be said about it; the Knowe stands in this lonely glen, aloof, green, and mysterious, the first faint, indecipherable scratch upon our palimpsest.

There is another scratch - of a date perhaps nearly the same as that of the Moat Knowe, perhaps very different, but equally uncertain - up in the hills a few miles beyond this glen. It consists of about a dozen low hummocks, in shape like blunt L's or hatchets, lying in a nearly flat piece of ground about the size of a couple of tennis courts. A generation ago they were very clear to the eye. To-day the combined depredations of grass, heather, sheep and draining have made it almost impossible for a stranger to detect them. They are supposed to be the remains of a primitive village of turf dwellings. They are as likely to be ancient places of burial. But, together with the Moat Knowe, they are the only remaining trace of evidence of who inhabited our valley and the surrounding hills before the first dawn of history.

Of the first impression made on this part of Scotland by the early Christian Church the traces are more numerous and more definite. St. Machar and St. Kieran, reputed two of the first Christian missionaries to evangelize Carrick and Galloway, left the district the legacy of their names, attached to more than one consecrated site. Indeed a study of the etymology of Carrick place-names seems to show that at some period the whole of this part of the country must have been studded with chapels, wayside shrines, and the dwellings of priests. Of the first colonization of this neighbourhood by the pioneers of Christianity we have two distinct and tangible memorials. One is the square outline of the foundations of a tiny chapel which once stood on the brink of a narrow and thickly-wooded glen half-way down the valley's south-eastern side. It used to be known by the simple name of 'the Lady Chapel,' and seems to have been a place of pilgrimage in pre-Reformation times. What remained of its walls was pulled down over a century ago, and the stones used, with mistaken piety, to build a kind of small family mausoleum in the village churchyard.

Not far from the old peel-tower, on a high slope which looks down to the sea, and commands a splendid view of the lower part of the valley, stands another memorial of the early missionaries. On this site also there once stood a chapel known as Machrikill or 'Machars shrine.' All trace of the chapel walls has long disappeared, but in the little clump of trees which marks the place there still stand two roughly-hewn blocks of stone of quite extraordinary interest. By comparison with similar relics at Iona and elsewhere, they have been identified as the bases of crosses. Each has the deep slot in its top which once held the foot of the cross; and the smaller of the blocks has in addition the outline of a cross rudely incised on one face of it.

After the days of the saints there comes a long gap in our valley's record. The only thing that helps to fill it is its nomenclature. All over Carrick the place-names are predominantly Gaelic. Curiously enough, the Gaelic strain in Ayrshire names weakens as you go northward through Kyle. Its strength in southern Ayrshire testifies to the old kinship of Carrick with Galloway, which, as Lord Hailes wrote in his *Annals of Scotland,* 'anciently comprehended not only the country now known by that name, and the stewartry of Kirkcudbright, but also the greatest part, if not the whole, of Air-shire.' Gaelic was the language widely spoken in Galloway up to the seventeenth century, and there can be no doubt that it survived in Carrick also for a considerable time. The fact that every river, every considerable hill, and every old house and farm bears a name of Gaelic derivation tells us something of the racial characteristics of Carrick's inhabitants during the Middle Ages. It is significant, also, that there seems to be no Norse element in local nomenclature at all, even along the coast.

The next clear writing on the parchment is a part of the story of Robert Bruce, who began in this neighbourhood his great campaign for the recovery of his kingdom. Turnberry, where he landed after his crossing from Arran, is only a few miles away, and when fresh English forces threatened him after his victory there, it was to the heights overlooking this valley that he retreated before he moved south into Galloway. On the topmost ridge of the long hill rising just south of the glen where the old tower stands, a line of mounds marks the site of Bruce's encampment, where he lay for several weeks. It was an admirable choice for such a refuge. The whole floor of the valley lay open below him, so that no hostile force could approach him unobserved, and behind him was a wild country, practically impassable to strangers, into which he could at any time make his retreat. The traces of the King's entrenchnents are very clearly to be seen even today; but it is difficult to find the entrance to a small cave in the steep western face of the hill which is traditionally indicated as another of his refuges. It opens on to a narrow ledge concealed by thick-growing stunted hawthorns, and is no larger than a fox's earth. Inside there must once have been comfortable room for several men, but the roof has partially collapsed, and the cave is now little more than a passage.

After the days of Robert I the marks of habitation on our valley become more frequent and more enduring. We have reached a kind of miniature Homeric age; when Carrick is full of warring lairds banded together under one or other of the great houses, when the Earls of Cassillis grow to such power as to be known as the 'the Kings of Carrick,' and when

> 'Twixt Wigtoun and the toun of Ayr
> And laigh doun by the Cruives of Cree,
> Nae man sall get a lodging there
> Unless he court with Kennedie.

This period, when every man whose wealth or dignity could support it fortified his dwelling, sprinkled the valley with stone houses or peels. The fragment in the glen is as much as remains to-day of any of them. The rest have either disappeared or become merged into succeeding buildings, sometimes large mansions, sometimes farms: only their names survive. But in the days of James V they were so numerous as to be a very noticeable feature of the scenery. *'Multis amanis villis cingitur'* was George Buchanan's description of the river four hundred years ago, when he lived not far from it as tutor to Gilbert, Earl of Cassillis; and the description might stand to-day, though there is not one of those pleasant houses which Buchanan would recognize in its present form.

Apart from buildings, it is difficult to decipher what the sixteenth and seventeenth centuries left to us. Under the last of the Stewarts the neighbourhood began to make its reputation for cattle and corn - *'pascuis fecunda'* says Buchanan, *'non infelix frumento.'* Men began to burrow into the hill-side on the north-west in search of the coal whose outcrops darkened the earth on the lower slopes; they established regular fords over the river and something of a road was made up the valley towards Ayr. Then came the terrible days of civil war when men killed each other for the sake of the King or the Covenant. Even in this little corner of Scotland there were sharp divisions. Most of the people were staunch Covenanters. The Maybole copy of the Covenant may be seen in the National Museum of Antiquities at Edinburgh and many of the names scrawled upon it are still among the commonest in the valley. Many of the inhabitants however were of the Episcopalian persuasion. The owner of the tower in the glen raised a troop of horse for Montrose - and here a line of writing on our parchment comes clear through the marking of later records. In 1827 - not so very long ago historically speaking - there died an old man who remembered seeing in his boyhood the remains of the banks constructed in a field near the river to form the temporary enclosure in which his great-great-great-grandfather kept the horses he gathered for the service of the King's Lieutenant-General in 1649.

The cavalier's son served the same cause in a much less honourable manner. In 1685 he guided a party of dragoons from a farm of his to a cottage a mile or two away where a certain zealous supporter of the Covenant lived. The man heard the approach of his enemies just too late and was shot while trying to make his escape through a window. The story is recorded in Wodrow's history, and the unfortunate Covenanter's tombstone keeps the memory of his betrayer unenviably green. The churchyard where it stands is a lovely spot, encircled with old trees. The church is now a ruin, but every year a service, known locally as 'the preaching,' is held in the churchyard in memory of the Covenant martyrs, known and unknown, of the parish. It is simple but indescribably impressive, and to see and hear it is to realize how strong, even to-day, is the recollection of 'the killing times,' Other traditions of those days hang about the valley. By the road that leads out of it towards Barr, for instance, stands a great boulder known by the name of 'Peden's Pulpit.' On a hill-top on the other side of the valley, a concealed hollow is pointed out as the place where conventicles used to be held. A few years ago, also, the directions of a bed-ridden old woman of eighty-five led me to discover the grave of two other Covenanters on the moor near the head of the glen where the Lady Chapel used to stand. Her brother, long since dead, 'aye used to gang there to read his Bible on a Sabbath afternoon.' After a good deal of search I found the small tilted stone which marked the spot; it bore four deeply-cut initials and the *memento mori* device of a skull and crossbones common on gravestones of the seventeenth and eighteenth centuries.

And so we come to the eighteenth century and the main inscription, save for a few erasures and insertions, on our parchment.

The great change in the face of Scottish landscapes, due to the advance in knowledge and practice of agriculture which was one of the principal features of Scotland's history in the eighteenth century, began comparatively early in Ayrshire. The peak of the change in our valley came in the 'seventies. The owner of most of the land in it, whose direction of its fortunes lasted from the year before George II died till two years before Waterloo, was a voluminous correspondent and an almost morbidly careful preserver of other people's letters to himself. As a result it is clearer to us than it could otherwise be that the aspect of the valley on which we look to-day is almost entirely his creation.

This laird completely transformed his estate. 'He drained, enclosed, and manured his fields, clearing them of stones some of which were so large that they had to be blown up with gunpowder. He opened a lime-quarry to increase the fertility of his fields - the huge caves left by the excavations still survive - established a rotation of crops, and experimented with grass-seeds. He imported English sheep to improve the breed of the native stock, He planted trees indefatigably on both sides of the valley. He laid out roads which to-day have become main highways to the neighbouring towns, and paths through all the most picturesque parts of the policies around his house. He built two really beautiful stone bridges over the river, as well as many smaller ones over burns, and he built a great many small houses and farm-buildings,which were up to the best standards of housing of his day. By the time he died there was little for his successor to do with the estate but to maintain it in the condition in which he left it. He had found the valley a half-tamed wilderness and left it a garden. Its beauty of today is largely the creation of that eighteenth-century laird. He made his little corner of Scotland neither a rich man's pleasance nor a market-garden, but the perfect mixture of productive utility and natural decoration: wood and field, road and river, blended in the landscape in ideal proportion and arrangement.

It is a green and seductive country, this valley. It has neither the bleakness of the north nor the luxury of the south. It is the loveliest place in Scotland, which is to say, in the world. But to me a large part of its fascination derives from the strong impression it produces on my mind of continuity with the past. I can hardly walk a mile through it in any direction without coming on some scene or some object that revives that impression. It may be one of the pretty little stone bridges made by that eighteenth-century laird over the burn which goes singing down the glen of the Lady Chapel. Or it may be no more than the old half-decayed pump to which, according to tradition, he used to walk every day to drink a cup of its water, and from which water was brought to him as he lay on his death-bed at the age of eighty-one. His letters, though his epistolary style was more correct than attractive, are most vivid when they speak of projects or improvements made on the estate, as for instance when they trace in detail the course to be taken by a new road, and discuss the adjustments which must be made in the line of a march to enable the road to complete its course without leaving its projector's property. After reading such pleasantly matter-of-fact details, set down in his beautifully formal handwriting, no walk along that road can ever again be dull, however well you may know every turn of it.

Then there was the coin dug up a year or two ago when a drain was being constructed across a field between a recently planted wood and the river. Somewhere in this neighbourhood, we knew, had stood one of the old houses to which Buchanan refers, but of which every trace but its name had vanished. It might have been anywhere within a circle as much as a quarter of a mile wide. But here, a couple of feet below the surface, this coin was turned up - a silver piece about the size of a florin; it was in good preservation, and was identified without much difficulty as a half-merk of James VI's time. We resumed the search for the site of the vanished house with renewed enthusiasm, for there seemed to be no reason except its proximity why that coin should have been dropped just there; and it was not long before we found, at the edge of the wood, the unmistakable outline of the old foundations.

But I think the most astonishingly vivid example I have ever known in this neighbourhood of the past surviving in the present was in a metaphor casually employed by the same old woman who told me of the Covenant martyr's grave. Its strangeness was the more striking in that not only did it obviously derive from the everyday speech of long before the Reformation but it occurred in the mouth of one living in a district where the spirit of that great change has always been particularly strong. The speaker was discussing a certain house not far from where she lived. It was remarked to her that it was too large a house to be comfortable. Ah, she replied, 'ye can aye sing a mass in each corner.'

2

The Kilkerran Improvers

I

Any bias in favour of the improving lairds noticeable in this book is frankly due to my own family history, for indeed I cannot but feel impressed by the record of the improvers and their contribution to the economy of rural Scotland when I see around my own home every day the visible achievement of a typical group of them in the development of the family estate. This central part of the valley of the Water of Girvan in Carrick, mostly comprised by the northern end of Dailly parish, is in its modern aspect largely the creation of three men: my great-great-grandfather, Sir James Fergusson, fourth baronet of Kilkerran, his uncle Sir Adam Fergusson, the third baronet, and Sir Adam's father Sir James, the second baronet but better known by his judicial title of Lord Kilkerran. The work of my father, grandfather and great-grandfather, apart from the continued development of the forestry side of the estate, has chiefly been to maintain and successively modernise the structure erected on Lord Kilkerran's foundations - for he, rather than his son and grandson, was the 'improver' in the strict historical sense of the word. From the family papers of himself and his immediate successors, amplified by the evidence of the landscape itself and of maps, can be deduced the story of one estate's development: an instance typical of many in Scotland [1] but from its familiarity to me the easiest to describe.

The history of Kilkerran is only one section of a considerable body of evidence refuting the assumption of textbook historians that the improvement of rural Scotland only began after the Jacobite rising of 1745 had been extinguished - as though the improvers, with some unexplained prescience, had held their hands until they were finally assured of tranquillity. There are many estates whose records prove the contrary, but such histories are often unpublished or, even when published, little read. Examples are Monymusk, where Sir Archibald Grant was building dykes, sowing grass and pease, and planting oaks and firs as early as 1719;[2] Penicuik, where Sir John Clerk the same year was 'bussied' about the plantations and nurseries on the banks of the Midlothian Esk which he had begun in 1709, and in the course of thirty years 'planted more than 300,000 trees';[3] and the many lairds whose improvements are discussed in the transactions of 'The Honourable the Society of Improvers in the Knowledge of Agriculture in Scotland', founded in 1723.

Kilkerran lies in a district which at the beginning of the eighteenth century was agriculturally as backward as the rest of Scotland but seems to have been well regarded by contemporaries. Its fertility had been praised generations before by the historian George Buchanan,[4] who spent some time in Carrick when he was tutor to Gilbert Kennedy, afterwards third Earl of Cassillis. A less friendly observer, an English spy who reported on Carrick between 1563 and 1566, but did not apparently venture more than a mile or two up the Girvan valley, dismissed it as 'a barrant cuntree but for bestiall;' adding, 'The people for the moste part speketht Erishe.'[5] But observers of the seventeenth century had commented admiringly on its 'plesant, lairge, and fruitfull wallages',[6] and 'adiacent little pretty greine hilles, intermingled with some hadder and mosse'.[7] The Rev. William Abercrummie, writing soon after 1690, [8] grew lyrical on the 'faire pleasant prospect' of the valley, whose 'many pleasant houses', the 'amoenae villae' commended by Buchanan, stood surrounded by gardens, orchards, woods and other 'accommodations'[9]. Macky, some twenty-five years later, also noted the district as 'a beautiful little vale for some miles'.[10] All this admiration had been inspired by the Girvan valley in its unimproved state - which, we may be sure, was pretty wild.

The lands which the future Lord Kilkerran and his descendants were to take in hand were not, for the most part, the old family estate of Kilkerran, which consisted of a few hill farms near the tall stone tower where the Fergussons had lived at least since the middle of the fifteenth century and probably a good while before that. He was not, indeed, in his early childhood, in the line of succession to the property, which had descended from his great-grandfather Sir John Fergusson - that hot-blooded cavalier whose mother had been the kinsman of Alexander Forrester of Garden, and who was later knighted by Charles I. In Lord Kilkerran's boyhood the laird of Kilkerran was his cousin Alexander (Sir John's grandson of the elder line), a man whom subsequent family tradition remembered as 'foolish', and who was cited for scandalous behaviour to 'compeir' before the kirk session of Dailly in 1699. Either the ordeal of Alexander's penance, from which he was not finally released for nearly a year, or the poverty to which he and his father had been reduced by the fines laid on the royalist Sir John, determined him to leave the parish - which meant leaving Kilkerran. He had already sold a good part of the family property in 1696, and in 1701 he parted with all that remained of it - 'the tower, fortalice, manors, lakes, houses, edifices, gardens, orchards, fishings,' and so forth. The purchaser of both lots was his first cousin, Mr John Fergusson of Barclanachan, advocate, the father of the future Lord Kilkerran.

Sir John Fergusson, who about 1650 had 'retired abroad till the Restauration, a short time after which he died',[11] had left, besides other children, a son named Simon or Simeon, of whom I can discover little, except that the Presbytery of Ayr included him with his father in their list of 'disaffected persons' (i.e. opposed to the Covenanters) in 1645.[12] Being a great-grandfather of Sir Adam Fergusson's, he was presumably that one at whom James Boswell, an illwisher of Sir Adam's, obscurely gibed as having been 'a messenger',[13] meaning, perhaps, a messenger-at-arms. He married Jean Craufurd, the daughter of Mr George Craufurd, minister of Kilbride, and he 'acquired the lands of Auchinwin and others, parts of the estate of Kilkerran, by adjudication led at his instance against his brother Alexander', [14] the father of the 'foolish' son. It may have been at Auchinwin, near Maybole, that Simon's grandson James was born in 1688.

Simon bought two small farms from the Earl of Cassilis in 1675 and died between 1691 and 1694. In 1686 John Fergusson, his son, began the recovery of the family fortunes. John's mother had, under her marriage contract, a 'locality' of Auchinwin, that is to say an appropriation to her in liferent of that property, and from this she had saved 'some thousand merks'. With this sum added to the proceeds of five years at the Bar, where he had been 'eminently successful',[15] John Fergusson was able to buy an old Kennedy property called Barclanachan (earlier, Balmaclanachan) which marched with the Kilkerran lands to the north.[16] It had been bought in 1684 by James Whitefoord of Dunduff,[17] whose daughter Jean John

Fergusson had married the same year.[18] No doubt, therefore, the young couple acquired it at a moderate price.

Robert Kennedy of Barclanachan, who was still alive in 1722, was the last of an old family which had held land of the Earls of Cassillis since before 1502.[19] The property which passed through the laird of Dunduff's hands to John Fergusson was mostly hill pasture, comprising the modern sheep-farms of Blair, Garleffin, Doughty and Dalwyne, besides two others which survive on the modern map only as the names of hills, Knockingalloch and Auchingairn. But on the west the high rolling expanse of coarse grass, heather and moss-hags dipped steeply down into the fertile Girvan valley; and here, half a mile from the river, stood the house of Barclanachan at the foot of curving hill-spurs whose concavity faced north-west. No description of it exists, but it was probably, like the few of its contemporary neighbours that survive, a tall L-shaped stone tower. From an inventory of the plenishing left in it at John Fergusson's entry, we know that it contained, like all such houses, a 'hall' and a 'chamber of deis', besides a 'brod chamber'. Abercrummie only mentions it briefly as 'the house of Barclanachan with its gardens and orchards all which are surrounded by wood, all the water from this downward till near Daillie being so covered with wood that it looks lyke a forrest';[20] and he includes it in a later passage among a list of 'mansion-houses all alongst Girvan which gives a very delightfull prospect to any who from the top of the hills, that guard the same, shall look downe upon that pleasant trough'.[21]

Some of the old house of Barclanachan was incorporated into that which John Fergusson erected, but his new house was thoroughly modern in character. Without, it was handsomely symmetrical: within, it was spacious, with high, well lighted rooms, simply panelled and (on the first floor) dignified by vaulted ceilings. Its appearance when first built must strongly have resembled that of Melville, designed at about the same time (1692) for the first Earl of Melville by James Smith, probably with the advice of Sir William Bruce.[22] It faced north, but that gave its main rooms a fine view across the valley, and moreover turned a protecting shoulder to the prevailing south-west winds which blew along the valley from the sea, 'coming up the bottom', as Lord Kilkerran wrote forty years later, 'as from a pipe or bellows.' It was to break the assault of these winds that John Fergusson planted in 1706 a belt of silver firs, which stand to this day, beyond the south side of the Barclanachan burn, on ground which he had got in tack in 1705 from his neighbour Alexander Kennedy of Drummellan.

The old tower of Kilkerran, whose name was transferred to the new Barclanachan, was abandoned after 1701, though time and weather needed another century and a half to bring it to ruin, and one lofty gable of it still stands. It was in 1701 that John Fergusson became the laird of Kilkerran. He had in 1696 bought a considerable parcel of the family estate, lying between Barclanachan and the old tower, from his cousin Alexander: the farms of Murestoun, Poundland, Glengie, Maldenoch and Ballibeg. Now in 1701 he acquired 'the £10 land of old extent of Kilkerran', with all the attached farms from 'Over and Nether Penbleath', above the head of the glen, down past Gettybeg, 'with the mill of the same,' to Balcamie near the new-built kirk of Dailly, with the holm between whose ditches and drystane dykes Sir John Fergusson had pastured the troop of horse he raised for Montrose.[23]

The sasine of 14 May 1701 proceeded on a charter from King William III erecting the estate, which former Fergussons had held of the Earls of Cassillis as superiors, into 'a free barony called the barony of Kilkerran'. With the charter and sasine the new laird acquired another document which established his title even beyond its strict legality. His outgoing cousins, as Nisbet recorded, 'Alexander the father, John and William the two sons, sign a separate writ, which was in my hands, by which they cheerfully renounce all interest and title they in any manner of way pretend to the above lands, and wishes a happy enjoyment to the said Sir John and his. Yet still' - the careful genealogist added - 'the primogeniture and right of blood, as heir-male, is in the person of William Fergusson of Auchinblain, who carries the ancient arms of the family'.[24]

'The said Sir John' did not enjoy that dignity in 1701; but it was not long delayed. He had now an eminent position at the Scots Bar; he was a considerable landed proprietor; and, even if lacking 'the primogeniture and right of blood', he was the territorial representative of a family which a former Lyon King of Arms had listed among 'the most ancient gentrey' of Carrick.[25] Thus he had become enough of a figure to be included among those whom Queen Anne's ministers thought it wise to recommend for the distribution of honours in the tense autumn of 1703 after the Scots Parliament had passed the Act of Security;'[26] and on St Andrew's Day of that year 'Magister Joannes Fergussone de Kilcarran' was created a baronet of Scotland. He matriculated a coat-of-arms in 1719.

Sir John took some part in public life in Ayrshire - he was agent for the town of Ayr in 1704 [27] and was appointed a Deputy Lieutenant for the county in 1715 - but I have found little record of his work as an improver. The rental-book, kept in his own hand, shows careful attention to the affairs of his estate; but it also illustrates how in his day agriculture in the valley was still primitive, even though potatoes had been grown in Dailly parish as early as 1697.[28] The rent of Murestoun, one of Sir John's best farms, as late as 1727 was only £120 Scots 'of siller rent', and the rest in kind-a stone of butter, a lamb, twelve hens and twelve chickens.

The first improvement of the estate was in afforestation; but this was not due to Sir John himself, despite the planting of the belt of silver firs in 1706 and of three groups of others in 1707 - which likewise still survive, grown to enormous size - in the deep shelter of the Lady Glen. This work was taken in hand by Sir John's eldest son James, who caught the mania for improvement at the early age of twenty-three. 'I came pretty early', he writes, 'to take a liking to planting, and which my father gave me full latitude in, tho' little disposed to it himself. ... I begun in the spring 1711 to sow for nurseries - the very year I was admitted advocat and came to live with my father in the country - and spring 1715 begun the hill planting and soon made great progress in it.' Besides planting for timber he improved the picturesque setting of the house, designing a 'great diagonal' of beeches to mount the slope of the bank behind it and clumps of others in well chosen spots around; and he considered opening up the view across the river which the natural wood 'lyke a forrest' obscured.

His letters to his newly wedded wife, Jean Maitland, grand-daughter of the fifth Earl of Lauderdale, a few months after their marriage, reveal the improver in his element, concerned for the moment not with agriculture but with amenity, and planning amiable little surprises for the partner to whom he was devoted but whom he had been obliged for the moment to leave with her mother and her first baby in Edinburgh. 'I am never within doors while it is fair', he writes; and, some days ... later,

'Our weather is so very bad that I get but very slow advances made in my projects tho' I do keep the lads pretty closs to work while they can stand out.' One letter goes into particulars on a new walk, and from their evidence its course was traced and uncovered some forty years ago; we know it to-day as 'Lady Jean's Walk'.

'I must now for your diversion (having nothing worth writing other to tell you) let you know what progress I have made in spite of the bad weather. I have made the walk I intended from the entry to the great bank up throw the old timber called the hag,[29] and pierced the view throw the park, and have when in the hag carried off a spiral walk which leads up to [the] head of it into the great diagonal which realy looks extreamly pretty. It['s] very natural and will I'm sure please you. I have near finished the little cover I intended for the rabbets by a little roofed house added to their former habitation in which they could not subsist in the winter time, and we have agreed for the building of a pidgeon house. I hope to find the pleasure of a pidgeon pye - you know when. This progres I have made amidst very bad weather which has cost the fellows many a wet skin tho' I belive their throats were not so oft wet as they would have been had my lamb been here, as they now and then say.'

Sir John Fergusson died, aged 75, on 14 February 1729, and was buried in the abandoned tower of Kilkerran. The last addition to the estate in his lifetime, which James bought in his name in 1728, was Dalduff, two miles up the river, once the home of a cadet branch of the Kilkerran Fergussons, and described by Abercrummie as 'a small stone house with ane orchard and good corne feilds about it'.[30] It was sold in 1946.

II

After Sir John's death his son continued the work of improving the estate with ardour and possibly now with more capital to finance it. One of his first cares, during the summer following his father's death, was to go carefully through the titles to various parts of the estate and get them correctly 'registrat', for Sir John 'had generally omitted to registrat his material writes', to the uneasiness of his more methodical son. Sir James made 'doubles' of all the inventories, one copy for the charter room at Kilkerran 'to be put up with the papers, and another to ly at Edinburgh'.

For a few years during the next decade it looked as if Sir James's energies might have to be directed away from the improvement of land. John, fifteenth Earl of Sutherland, Lady Jean's maternal grandfather, died in June 1733, and his grandson and successor, William, Lord Strathnaver, had to vacate the seat for the county of Sutherland which he had occupied in the House of Commons for six years. In March 1734 [31] Sir James Fergusson became member for Sutherland in his place. The seat was virtually in the gift of the reigning Earl of Sutherland, being unique in that the qualified Sutherland voters were freeholders holding land not, as in other Scottish counties, of the King but of the Earl of Sutherland. It was natural that the new Lord Sutherland should choose his cousin to succeed him, for the old Earl had treated Fergusson with great friendliness and turned frequently to him for legal advice on rather delicate family matters. But Sir James was no mere tame nominee. He had high principles and a strong sense of public duty, and though he was member for Sutherland for only a few months the reputation clung to him ten years later of having 'by his own activity and merit got into Parliament'.[32]

It was another promotion that obliged him to retire from Westminster. He had hoped for a judge's gown since at least March of 1730, when Lord Kimmerghame died.[33] But it was not till 7 November 1735 that he was raised to the Bench in place of the deceased Lord Ormistoun and took his seat in the Court of Session as Lord Kilkerran. This automatically made him incapable of remaining in the Commons, under a clause which Sir Robert Walpole and Lord Islay (later third Duke of Argyll) had, in March 1734, inserted into a bill dealing with elections, for the sole purpose of excluding from Parliament James Erskine, Lord Grange. The clause might be, as its principal victim said, 'as ridiculous as to bring bombs and cannon to batter down a silly cottage';[34] but it was passed, and brought the whole race of Scottish political judges to an end which on the whole need not be regretted. Among its early effects was the abrupt termination, twenty months later, of Sir James Fergusson's Parliamentary career. Possibly he resented it. It might well have been some sense of filial loyalty that made his eldest son rather pointedly refuse to meet Walpole nine years later.[35]

Anyway, Lord Kilkerran now had the more time to devote to rural affairs. In 1736 he achieved an ambition of more than twenty years' standing by the purchase of Drummellan, the estate lying between the former Barclanachan and the river. Its proximity had hitherto prevented any improvement schemes to the west of the house, which stood on the very march of Drummellan. David Kennedy of Drummellan, who lived in the house of Drumburle on the far side of the Water of Girvan, nearly opposite Drummellan, had approached Sir James in 1731, supported by his wife's uncle, Robert Kennedy of Pinmore, with a proposal to sell 'the High and Laigh Mains'; and some months later, 'just as I was upon the wing for the winter session,' with a larger proposal. 'Drummellan was at a pinch: sell to some body he must'; and although he and his advisers drove harder and harder bargains with each successive piece of ground sold, the upshot was that by 1736 Lord Kilkerran had bought all the land down to the riverside.

'The purchase', he wrote, 'was the dearest, I doubt, was ever made in Carrick. Yet considering the conveniency of it to me, I may say necessity of it, to make the place tolerable, had I omitted the opportunity, I should never have forgiven myself. ... I might have had it much cheaper, but ... it continues a satisfaction to me that I had it without a grudge, on the contrary that my getting of it made the man to think himself happy when he parted with it.' As with the acquisition of Kilkerran itself, gain had been sweetened by goodwill on both sides.

This purchase had considerable results, on both the amenity and the agriculture of the estate. First, Lord Kilkerran was able to layout a garden to the west of his house. All vestige of it has long disappeared except one ancient cherry-tree which blossoms gloriously every spring, but the grass-park covering its site is still named the Pleasure Grounds. Hitherto the prospect from Lord Kilkerran's western windows had been unsightly. 'The constant [passage] to Drummellan for horse and foot had past memory been down through the meadows summer and winter, keeping especially in winter no fixed road, which could not well be in so potchy a ground. This must have been an eye sore had it been mine.'

Further, the purchase of Drummellan stimulated Lord Kilkerran's agricultural improvements. 'But for my first purchase of the part above the highway I do not think I should ever have dream'd of inclosing my own muir, the conveniency of stone for inclosing on the march between my new purchase and Glengie having been the first thing that put it in my head.'

The enclosures on the moor above the house amounted to some 500 acres. Lord Kilkerran experimented with 'paring, burning, and liming', using lime from a quarry on his farm of Blair, a mile up the hill above Kilkerran, to get rid of the 'hadder and mosse' characteristic of the district and establish good grass. 'I am well informed', wrote Robert Maxwell of Arkland, in the transactions of the Society of Improvers, 'that ... the common farmers in the neighbourhood, who, until they saw what he did, and what crops he got, never so much as once fancied that such barren-like ground was a subject proper for agriculture, begin now to copy after him.'[36]

No improver could wish for a better epitaph. The heartbreak of some improvers was the difficulty of getting their tenants to forsake their traditional, laborious and unremunerative methods of husbandry. One of the earliest pamphlets published by the Society of Improvers was addressed particularly to farmers who objected to the introduction of summer fallowing 'that they are poor, and cannot forego the want of a crop, and one crop cannot be expected to make up the loss of two'.[37] At Drummond Castle the Duke of Perth, when he attempted to introduce summer fallowing and the sowing of artificial grasses, found that his tenants 'disliked everything new' and 'regarded these essays as the freak of the day, and of the same stamp with race or hunting horses'.[38] Cockburn of Ormistoun, who studied the advantage of his tenants 'equal at least to the making the estate better to those who shall come after me, and I am sure much more than any advance of the rent to myself,' complained of 'the obstinate stupidity of our people - who talk of being good countrymen but act against anything can improve it'.[39] Similarly in Mull and Morven the people were described in 1732 as 'bewitched' in their adherence to the wasteful old methods of agriculture.[40] At Monymusk Sir Archibald Grant wrote vigorous exhortation to his backward tenants: 'Such of you as are diligent misapply it and won't take advice from those who know better, nor will you follow good example when you see it has good effects, but will keep straitly to the old way. But also a great many of you are idle and trifle away a good deal of your time. ... As to your poor living I am sorry for it, but it is your own fault. For God's sake, then, be roused by the example of others and by your own reason to pursue your true interest.'[41] At Kilkerran the first improver made at least a breach in the old conservatism. It was left to his son and successor to widen it.

Lord Kilkerran's lifetime brought also many improvements to the inside of the family home. Being a modern house, it was probably never other than dignified and cheerful, and it is hard to fit it into the squalid picture of country life in the early eighteenth century rather overdrawn by Henry Grey Graham. Still, there can have been few pictures on its walls in Sir John's time, when 'artists had scanty encouragement from gentlemen who were too poor to pay for pictures and too uncivilised to care for them';[42] and there were so few books in the house that during his years as an advocate Lord Kilkerran had occasionally borrowed from the well-filled shelves of the minister of Kirkmichael, Mr James Lawrie.[43]

Lady Jean, however, having been an only child, brought some quite good portraits of her Lauderdale and Sutherland relations into the family; and a few years before his death Lord Kilkerran had himself and two of his daughters, Jean and Peggy, admirably painted by Ramsay. The girls' portraits are signed and dated 1752, so that if the judge's portrait in his robes as a Lord of Justiciary belongs to the same year it shows him as he was when he took his probably uneasy seat beside the Duke of Argyll on the bench at Inveraray for the Appin murder trial. It is much to be regretted that Lady Jean did not sit to Ramsay too - probably because two portraits of her, neither of much merit, hung in the house already.

Lord Kilkerran also began the formation of a library, later to be notably enlarged by his son Adam. As might be expected of 'one of the ablest lawyers of his time',[44] he collected many volumes on law; but others on history, theology and agriculture - among the last a handsome copy of the 1706 edition of John Evelyn's *Silva* - also bear his bookplate with the beautifully engraved coat-of-arms closely modelled on the design of that in Nisbet's *System of Heraldry*.

Of the furniture of his time little has survived in the house except a set of embroidered chairs bearing the initials of Lady Jean and three of her daughters, who worked their now faded but still graceful flowers.

Though writing of Lord Kilkerran mainly as an improver, I must spend a little space on his personal character, of whose 'probity and integrity' the tradition lingered long.[45] The family correspondence, some of which I have published elsewhere, shows an unusually affectionate and intimate family circle, whose children address their father not with the formal 'Honoured Sir' of the period but as 'Dear Pappa'. Among the earlier letters are a few from 'the old folks', Sir John and his lady, proud and happy in their successful son, their 'dear daughter' his wife, and their 'litil comrade' the eldest grandson. A generation later Lord Kilkerran appears both as an earnest and as an indulgent father, adjuring one son to make the best use of his years of study, lest he 'return ... a mere country squire',[46] and trusting another with absolute freedom of responsibility in both route and expenditure when making the grand tour.'[47]

Outside the family, too, he seems to have been a congenial companion. Lord Auchinleck 'met with Lord Kilkerran and Baron Maule in a club' one summer evening in Edinburgh, and a year later spent some jolly hours with the same companions in 'the Duke's new inn' at Inveraray, where the wine was 'excellent' and Lord Kilkerran (then in his 68th year) 'drunk several bumpers in high spirits and tho' I remonstrated to him privatly against his doing it woud not refrain, and to this I impute a threatning of the gout which prevented his going to the Court at Glasgow and made him leave me the second day of the circuit'.[48] John Maule of Inverkeilor, one of the Barons of the Court of Exchequer, would have been a kindred spirit very likely to move Kilkerran to conviviality, for he was as enthusiastic a tree-planter in Angus as the other in Ayrshire.[49]

The gout Lord Kilkerran owed to such occasions so tormented his hands and feet that he had sometimes to dictate his letters and throughout his judicial career could not walk further than the garden he had made before his house. But his brain was active to the end of his life, and his kindliness extended far beyond his family circle. The second son of the harassed minister of Kirkmichael owed to Lord Kilkerran's patronage[50] the bursary that launched him on a successful career; and a tattered

1. The old road from Girvan to Maybole,
near the Black Cock Inn.

2. Ox-bow lakes, remnants of the course of the Water of
Girvan before it was straightened.

3. Kilkerran nestles in the valley side.

4. 'The little possession of the Ruglen' - the former Smithy

notebook once belonging to the tenant of one of the outlying Kilkerran farms testifies that he was a lenient landlord.

III

Lord Kilkerran died at his little house just outside Edinburgh on 20 January 1759, and his death was notable news as far away as Kelso.[51] The heir to the estate and baronetcy of Kilkerran was his second son Adam, John the eldest, an amiable and promising young soldier, having died of a tuberculous complaint in 1750.

Sir Adam, whose education at Edinburgh University had been enlarged by nearly three years of continental travel, spent his early years at the Scots Bar and his prime in Parliament as member for Ayrshire. A diligent, honourable, cultivated and kindly man, he was unshakably orthodox in all that he did, and might stand as the regular type of all conscientious Lowland lairds of the middle and late eighteenth century. He did his sober duty to his county and his country, farmed and planted assiduously, lent his countenance and aid to innumerable beneficent projects, and enriched Kilkerran with many pictures and books in the best taste of his time, if not always such as posterity might wish him to have chosen. Methodical in everything, he preserved most letters that he received, and generally a 'scroll' of his answer to each. The impression left by every record of his long and well spent life is one of invincible correctitude.

At a time when 'swearing was thought the right, and the mark, of a gentleman',[52] Sir Adam was sufficiently remarkable for his restraint of language to earn from Burns the epithet of 'aith-detesting'.[53] An old woman who as a child had once seen Sir Adam in a temper described to my father how "Sir Adam cam out and he chappit on the grund wi' his stick, and says he, 'Dinna think that because I'm no swearin I'm no angry.'"

Not a single sentence in Sir Adam's voluminous correspondence suggests that he ever made a joke in his life; but another anecdote preserved by local tradition hints at a dry humour on occasions. Calling for the first time on his new tenant of the farm of Whitehill, Sir Adam asked abruptly of the woman who opened the door, 'Is Couper in?'

'*Mr* Couper', replied the goodwife to the stranger in a reproving tone, 'is no at hame.'

'Weel,' said Sir Adam mildly, 'tell him Adam Fergusson was speirin for him' - and turned on his heel.

Serious or not, he was certainly an amiable personage. His early correspondence and account-book, during the grand tour which he began with George Dempster, his lifelong friend, and just after it, show that he led a reasonably gay social life, was well read, had good taste and judgment, and was by no means narrow-minded. An effusive young lady who was a guest at Kilkerran soon after he returned from his grand tour has preserved a partial but engaging picture of him, noted one October Sunday when bad weather had prevented the house-party from going to church at Dailly. She had formed one of the family circle 'all seated with decency and composure hearing a sermon read by so noble a youth as the eldest son of Lord K-'. She described Adam as 'genteel in his person, easie in his address, totally void of foppery or affectation, idolized by his parents, admired by everybody that know him', an attentive son and affectionate brother, 'sensible and sedate yet so chearful, upon occasions even gay, having seen so much yet never seeking opportunities of discovering his knowledge, acknowledged a fine scholar without the least tincture of pedantry' - and a great deal more to the same effect, the whole suggesting a kind of Sir Charles Grandison, for the diarist was very evidently a devoted reader of Richardson.[54]

Evidently Adam at 25 was well fitted to ensnare a young lady's heart. But he was anything but romantic himself, and can never have been frivolous. Maturity certainly sobered him still more; and 'enthusiasm', that bugbear of the orthodox Georgian, was abhorrent to him. Between him and the volatile James Boswell there was a natural and unconquerable antipathy, despite their early acquaintance and the long friendship of their fathers. The dislike for him recorded several times in James Boswell's journals and occasional writings seems to have been fixed by Sir Adam's evasion of a subscription-list for Corsican relief which 'Corsica Boswell' was pressing on his acquaintance in 1769[55]; but Boswell's violent zeal for the Douglas side in the great Douglas Cause had already estranged him from the advocate who had prepared the Hamilton 'memorial'. Jealousy of Sir Adam's long tenure of the Ayrshire seat in Parliament was certainly an ingredient, and appears very strongly in a venomous letter on Ayrshire politics which Boswell contributed to the *Public Advertiser* of 27 July 1785, in which he observed that it was 'very disagreeable ... to be obliged to descend from recording the wisdom and wit of Dr JOHNSON to a contest about *Sir Adam Fergusson*'.[56]

Not that Sir Adam could not like and be liked by those of far different temperament to his own. 'You never appear to me more amiable,' wrote the versatile and speculative George Dempster, 'than when I see your grave face and sound head prepared to blow all my speculations into the air from whence they came'.[57] Sir Adam's interests were wide. In his young days he had even been one of the group of Edinburgh gentlemen who subscribed to send James Macpherson into the Highlands in search of the presumed 'epic' that afterwards appeared as 'Fingal'[58] and more than a quarter of a century later he took the trouble to collect an old Gaelic poem himself in Skye.[59] In 1768 he was chosen Lord Rector of Glasgow University in opposition to Adam Smith.[60] His friends included men of such widely various distinction as his brother-in-law the learned Lord Hailes, William Nairne (later Lord Dunsinnan), the dull but diligent Sir John Sinclair of Ulbster, and 'Fish' Craufurd. Among his Ayrshire neighbours, the only one between whom and Sir Adam there was a coldness seems to have been David, tenth Earl of Cassillis, who owned a good deal of the land across the river from Kilkerran.

Their hostility was originally political, for Sir Adam won the Ayrshire seat in Parliament in 1774 as the candidate of a group of independent gentlemen against the combined interest of three powerful peers, Cassillis, Eglinton and Loudoun. David Kennedy of Newark, the sitting member, was their candidate[61]: the brother of the ninth Earl of Cassillis, whom he succeeded the following year. Sir Adam's success was unexpected. It 'vexed' Boswell enough to make him lose some sleep.[62] To Kennedy it may well have been much more irritating. He had further ground for annoyance when he succeeded not only to his brother's title and estates, and to the task of rebuilding Culzean to the new and splendid designs of Robert Adam, but also to an unfortunate dispute upon which a mass of Sir Adam's papers, docketed with references to 'the coal cause', dwells in wearisome detail.

On the long hill forming the north-west side of the Girvan valley, a former Earl of Cassillis had acquired the lands once owned by the monks of Crossraguel Abbey, which included some coal workings.[63] By 1775 Sir Adam also owned property along the slope of the hill and had planted trees there to the extent of 'near an hundred acres'. The coal under the surface remained, however, Cassillis property, and the workings, on what was still Cassillis ground, were let to a tacksman named Cumming. In 1749 [64] part of the workings had caught fire, and they continued to burn intermittently underground for many years. Expert opinion considered a closure of the workings the best if not the only way to smother the fire, and Sir Adam employed men to fill up the old Dalzellowlie pit on his ground, and planted the blackened slopes above it, 'labouring many years', as he said, 'to convert a nusance and a deformity into a beauty'.

Cumming, however, rashly continued to work the coal on Lord Cassillis's ground. He 'was in desperate circumstances and probably did not care what mischief he did, provided he made a little profit to himself'. He pushed his operations up to and under the march, and in the autumn of 1775 the fire broke out once more on the surface and destroyed four or five acres of Sir Adam's planting. Sir Adam took legal action to stop him. 'To my surprise', he wrote, 'the matter was taken up in the name of Lord Cassillis, and the bill of suspension was opposed for his Lordship by his counsel and agents.'

At this point Sir Adam happened to depart to spend the winter in Bath, and on 30 November, Thomas, ninth Earl of Cassillis, died. But the machine of the law ground its unrelenting way onward, and its unsympathetic progress provided the not unnatural cause of the new Earl's grievance. A long and bitter sentence in a letter he wrote to Sir Adam on 8 January 1776 explains it:

'Was it kind or like a neighbour to send a messenger with four or five attendants to my brother's house when his disease was hasting fast to the fatal period to which it came, and to send again the same disagreeable objects a few days before his death, and as if intended to make my misery more compleat to rouse me from that melancholy I was so justly under, with a summons against myself upon the morning of the day immediatly after my brother's interment?'

Sir Adam apologised for this unfeeling procedure for which he had not been responsible, but stuck to his resolve to have his trees protected. His determination was not unreasonable. By the summer of 1777 the fire had 'most sensibly advanced towards Tradonnock' so that there was 'no passing that way for smoke'. 'The coal cause' dragged on for nearly two years. The fire smouldered yet in Lord Cassillis's memory in 1779 [65]; and in the hill itself it burned long after both he and Sir Adam were in their graves, still emitting spasmodic smoke and gas within living memory. To this day, although the fire has long been extinguished, and coal is no more worked on the scene of the quarrel, the name of 'the Burning Hill' persists.

Sir Adam continued his planting. By the time he retired from Parliament in 1796, had his portrait nobly painted by Raeburn, and settled down for his old age, still a bachelor, with his eldest sister Jean to keep house for him, he had transformed the valley with 'about 400 Scots acres' of trees.[66] By the end of the century he had bridged the river at Drumgirnan ford, and carried a new road from it up on to the Burning Hill to join the old road to Maybole, running along its lower slopes above the valley which was now all reclaimed from the swamps and thickets of a hundred years earlier. In his old age he could look round upon his work and call it good.

He could have desired, for he could conceive, no better heritage than Kilkerran. 'I am convinced', he wrote, 'that there is not a climate to be found superior to this here, taking the whole year round (I wish, however, I could be relieved of the spring).' And again, one January, 'My opinion, founded on long experience, most certainly is, that there is not probably a milder air in the winter months than that in which I now sit' - in Great Britain, he meant, for he was discounting the claims of Devon. If the south-westerly gales sometimes brought down an old tree or two, Sir Adam did not complain. 'I believe', he observed, 'upon a moderate computation, for everyone blown down, I plant 5000.'

From the windows of Kilkerran, or as he rode to church at Dailly, where his old friend Mr Thomas Thomson the minister[67] had 'corn and clover fields in excellent order, and hedges growing vigorously',[68] Sir Adam could survey the improvements of his earlier years. Unlike his father, he had begun not with planting the hills but with reclaiming the bottom of the valley, whose fertile soil had in his youth been still covered with 'natural woods of oak and birch'.[69] He has left a valuable account of these operations in a letter to Andrew Wight,[70] who surveyed and reported on the improvements in many parts of Scotland in the late 1770's, but failed to find Sir Adam at home when he visited Kilkerran. The district struck Wight, when he entered it up the road from the south, as 'a narrow, but pleasant valley, of a good soil. ... There,' he wrote, 'in different fields, I saw various operations of husbandry carried on with industry and attention. The inclosures in perfection, both hedges and stone walls. Lime is the only manure used. I saw a number of sheep in a large inclosure opposite to the house, of different kinds, Dorchester, Cully, Bakewell, and also the breed of the country' - presumably blackface. Wight described 'the progress of agriculture in that part of the country' as 'chiefly owing to Sir Adam himself', thus echoing the tribute paid to Lord Kilkerran by Maxwell of Arkland thirty-five years before.

In his letter to Wight, Sir Adam recalled his memory of the countryside 'when there was scarce an inclosure in it but some few round the gentlemen's seats, when there was not a pound of grass seed sown from one end of it to the other, and when the whole attention of the farmer, and the whole dung of the farm, was applied to a few acres, while the rest was totally neglected.

'With regard to myself,' continued Sir Adam, 'my object has been to turn the farms in my own possession into good grass as soon as possible.' He described how he had blasted the erratic boulders in the holms with gunpowder, cleared the fields 'of shrubs and bushes', drained them, limed them at the rate of 'an hundred bolls to the Scots acre', and introduced a proper rotation of crops. Despite the Dorchester and Bakewell flocks, he professed himself dubious of the prospects of 'the English sheep in our hills'. He believed in the native breeds of both sheep and cattle. 'The utmost length that I think it would be safe to go, would be to endeavour to raise our own breed by a mixture with the English; and even that should be done with great caution'.

Regarding his tenants, Sir Adam was somewhat sparing of his praises. But he conceded that several deserved commendation 'for their attention and industry', and that there was 'a remarkable alteration to the better, both in their knowledge and management, since I began to attend to country affairs'. They were now all keen on proper enclosures, were 'getting into the practice, more or less, of sowing grass seeds', and, above all, 'the distinction of croft and field land, except among some of the poorest sort, is, in a manner, entirely abolished'.

This last was a notable step forward. Only fourteen years before, a Scottish agricultural writer had described the old system of infield and outfield in terms suggesting that it was still normal.[71] At Kilkerran Sir Adam's progressive measures had already relegated it to the past, partly by taking as some of his tenants 'farmers of great skill in husbandry' and partly by giving all his tenants long leases binding them to modern methods of manuring and cropping.[72] By 1794 the result of his and his father's policy had contributed to increase the valued rent of Dailly parish to more than three times that of thirty years earlier, and farm servants' wages, over sixty years, from six to nine times. 'The rising wages of common labour and domestic service', observed Mr Thomson in drawing up the 'Statistical Account' of the parish, 'ought, by an indifferent spectator, to be regarded as one of the happiest effects of increasing industry and opulence.'[73] In another part of Ayrshire another minister remarked that despite the steady rise in wages the price of oatmeal, 'the chief article of living, is nearly, at an average, the same it was 20 or 30 years ago.'[74]

For many years Sir Adam wrote regularly to his nephew and destined heir, James Fergusson, who after some years in India as a junior partner in the firm of Fergusson and Fairlie of Calcutta returned to Scotland in 1799 with the recommendation of one of his seniors that 'a nobler young man is not within my acquaintance'. A few months after his return James married his cousin Jean, the second daughter of Sir David Dalrymple, Lord Hailes, who had married one of Sir Adam's sisters. The same year he joined the Ayrshire and Renfrewshire Militia, who were employed in coastal defence in various parts of England during the period when Napoleon threatened invasion. James had risen to command them by 1807, but retired in June, his health being uncertain, and took a house in Essex, Thoby Priory; he lived there till 1810, when he settled in George's Square, Edinburgh. His first wife died after less than four years of marriage, and in December 1804 he married Henrietta Duncan, daughter of the admiral who was the victor of Camperdown. His first wife bore him three children, and his second thirteen.

Sir Adam's rather long-winded letters to his nephew contain much good advice, a few reflections on current political and military affairs, occasional reminiscences of his own career, and numerous details about the affairs of Kilkerran estate. He shows an avuncular interest in James's large family and sometimes offers tentative and tactful advice concerning their health or education. One of his last letters, written when he was over eighty, embraces some reflections on the distant past, the present and the future of Kilkerran, yet barely allows any glimpse into the inner mind of the undemonstrative man who had been so careful a steward of the heritage he had administered for over half a century. Age had not diminished his shrewdness or his realism.

He recommended James to try to acquire the remainder of the Burning Hill from Lord Cassillis - this was the twelfth Earl, afterwards first Marquess of Ailsa. The fire in the hill still persisted. 'That his Lordship will attempt working the coal in its present state and while the fire lasts, I think impossible ... That there are two seams of coal in the upper part of the hill which the fire has not touched I have good reason to believe.[75] These cannot be wrought while the fire continues: but when it is extinguished, which it must be in time, there will be nothing to hinder these two seams from being wrought; in other words the whole planting up as far as the nursery being destroyed. It is to that event that I look forward; and as it is for the family and for posterity that I am acting, I cannot but consider the acquisition of the coal, though of little consequence in the present circumstances, to be more material for the future prospect.'

There was also 'the little possession of the Ruglen', an island of Cassillis property on the lower slope of the hill some distance below the coal workings, which Sir Adam felt should be acquired, and one or two other farms of which he had not gained complete possession. 'My grandfather', he told James, 'purchased the superiority of part of his estate from the curators of John [eighth] Earl of Cassillis[76] at the beginning of the last century. He would have got the whole for the asking, as the affairs of that family were then embarrassed; but mist the opportunity. This my father has often regretted to me; but said that he had always abstained from speaking about it to his father, as he saw that he reproached himself with the neglect. This, I own, has always given me a strong desire to have these superiorities ... The acquisition ... would make me the immediate vassal of the crown in the whole estate, with the exception of one farm, Tradonnock, which holds of Sir Hew Hamilton, and which therefore you would have little difficulty to acquire.'[77] Sir Adam suggested that Lord Cassillis might be persuaded to exchange Ruglen for 'a slip of land' owned by Kilkerran on the north side of Mochrum Hill in Kirkoswald parish, 'quite out of sight from every quarter but from the leading entry to Culzean ... But,' the old man concluded, 'as my personal concern in the matter is very small, I should not wish to enter into any transaction, without your concurrence, in which you have so much more concern than myself.'

Though occasionally troubled by the gout, but to nothing like the same extent as his father, Sir Adam was still active enough at seventy-nine to go on a visit to Ulster with some of his nieces who wanted to see the Giant's Causeway. His last years must have had their lonely moments, for all his contemporaries in the family were now dead except his brother Lord Hermand. But the Fergusson and Dalrymple nieces often visited him at Kilkerran, and James's sister Kitty settled down there to look after her uncle in the summer of 1812.

He was very ill that winter, and did not live to see another. During his last illness in September 1818, his servant Primrose, according to family tradition, fetched his drinking-water every day from his favourite spring. He died early in the morning of the 25th, James, who had been summoned by express, arriving just too late to see him. 'We have few such men among us,' wrote Robert Jamieson the antiquary some months later, adding that Sir Adam 'almost seemed to belong to another age, and another state of society, more perfect than that we live in';[78] and the Scots Magazine published a warm eulogy of 'this venerable and respectable baronet'.[79]

IV

Sir James Fergusson, who succeeded his uncle at the age of 38, added one more chapter to the Kilkerran improvements, but he acted much more impulsively and in some respects less prudently than his uncle and grandfather. The inheritance of a large and by now very prosperous estate seems to have gone somewhat to his head, which was little more business-like than that of his father Charles, who had died in 1804, and whose financial misadventures had caused Sir Adam a good deal of worry. At all events, finding his income some five times what it had formerly been, Sir James embarked almost at once on extensive operations which were far beyond his means. Sir Adam had never spent more than £2,000 a year, including not only his household and personal expenses but also 'the large sum which keeping up and improving this place requires'. Sir James poured out his income and drew on his credit with such carefree enthusiasm that two years after his succession he found himself deep in debt to the tune of £70,000.

'I own I did not anticipate it', wrote his uncle Lord Hermand, to whom he applied for advice. 'Still, I do not wish to look back, though I must own there is something mysterious about the whole business.' His advice was to the point. Sir James must satisfy his creditors by putting himself into the hands of trustees, establish a sinking fund to pay off his debts, and live on fifteen hundred a year till they were discharged. 'This residue may appear small, and certainly is not adequate to a great establishment of servants, and other articles of luxury. Neither will it afford the erection of buildings and gardens, extremely proper in an estate of £10,000 a year, but nowise suited to present circumstances.' But this residue, added the judge with characteristic directness, would allow Sir James 'to bring up his numerous family as other families just as good have been brought up'. The probable alternative was for the creditors to arrest the rents of the estate, or the owner's liferent of it - 'and how he is to support his family in the mean time, I cannot form even a conjecture'.

Sir James, presumably, had to agree, for his affairs were somehow straightened out a good while before his death in 1888; but an endorsement of his on one of Lord Hermand's later letters suggests that he grumbled at first a good deal at the discipline which he was obliged to undergo.

The changes brought about by his expenditure were certainly considerable. He enlarged the house, employing the stones of the ruined tower of Drummellan,[80] and built two round-ended wings on to its western face, to which he transferred the main entrance. One wing contained a handsome drawing-room and a vast kitchen below it. In the opposite one were two large nurseries to house the growing tribe of young Fergussons. Sir James also threw the old garden to the west of the house into grass and laid out a new walled garden of some five acres half a mile away to the north. In the new fashion, he enclosed his policies, and in the old he continued to plant woods. But outside the private grounds he, too, made his contribution to the improvement of the valley and the progress of Ayrshire farming.

Less than a month after Sir Adam's death Sir James was writing of his plans to layout a new road up the valley towards Maybole in co-operation with three neighbouring lairds, Sir Hew Hamilton of Bargany, Quintin Kennedy of Drummellan (from whose grandfather Lord Kilkerran had bought most of the Drummellan lands), and James Fergusson of Crosshill, Principal Clerk of Session.[81] The last of these was an enthusiastic improver who fifteen years before had helped Sir Adam Fergusson and Thomas Kennedy of Dunure to plan the road from Maybole to the Garpin bridge over the Water of Girvan. [82] The projected new road was to join up with it at the Garpin bridge - where the modern village of Crosshill was built some years later - 'keeping generally the opposite side of the river from the present road and which now intended line will be mostly quite flat instead of going over the top of every hill as at present.' Besides the promoters, 'the public', Sir James added, 'will also be materially benefited.' The claim was well justified, since the project resulted in what is to-day the main public road up the valley from opposite Kilkerran to Crosshill. Sir James contributed to his share of the road a handsome stone bridge where it crossed the river, which was completed in 1825 and named Hamilton Bridge in compliment to his friend Sir Hew.

This performance, like some others, maybe set to Sir James's credit against his early extravagances, in reference to which old George Dempster wrote banteringly to him on 28 December 1813, while Sir James and his wife were spending a gay winter in Edinburgh, 'I assume some authority over Lady Fergusson, and must restrict her ladyship to one dinner, three routs, and two balls, and one supper in the 24 hours. It would be a proof of insanity, if a K.B. and his lady did not run stark, staring mad, for six weeks every winter.'

Before Sir James was brought up short by his debts he must at least have begun many other schemes. Some were abortive, like his attempt, against the advice Sir Adam had given him, to resume working the coal in the Burning Hill. He tried to extinguish the still stubborn fire underground by flooding it. 'The plan,' observed Lord Hermand in a letter of 1 November 1814, 'was I believe formerly tried, but failed from the number of fissures in the half calcined wastes. I fear you may have the same obstacle to encounter.'

A much more successful undertaking, which has proved highly beneficial to farming in the parish, was another joint operation between Sir James and Thomas Francis Kennedy of Dunure, and consisted of the straightening and embanking of the river's course between Sir Adam's bridge at Drumgirnan and Kennedy's house of Dalquharran, near the village of Dailly. Hitherto the river had coiled and meandered between the holms, cutting its corners at every spate and leaving the meadows waterlogged for half the summer. To-day sleek Ayrshire cows graze or fields of golden oats ripple in the breeze where once lay stagnant pools, and only in seasons of heavy rain does the water fill the curved depressions to indicate the windings of the old bed. Sir James had suggested 'laying back the banks' to Sir Adam in 1810, when Sir Adam replied that he himself had 'revolved it' in his mind, adding, 'The objection does not lye so much in the expence as in not knowing what could be done with so prodigious a quantity of earth as would have to be disposed of, and which cannot be carried to a distance.'

Tile-draining had been introduced into the parish by Mr Kennedy at Dalquharran, 'a most important improvement, 'and Sir James adopted it, too, during the last years of his life. Once again the example of the laird led the way in an agricultural reform, for after Sir James had begun tile-draining in his own fields he was 'followed in it by one of his principal tenants'. [83]

With the curbing of the Girvan's waters, the last major improvement to the estate was completed. Sir James helped to found the still flourishing Ayrshire Agricultural Society in 1835, and died three years afterwards, leaving Kilkerran to the less grandiose but more prudent management of his eldest son Charles, of whose wedding-day in 1829, which Sir James attended in a red coat, there is a glimpse in the pages of Lord Cockburn.[84] Sir Charles added to the estate in 1845 the small property of Drumburle, across the river, the last fragment of the former Drummellan lands.

But for the appearance of the railway, which came down from Ayr twenty years later, the absorption of some small holdings on the hillsides into larger farms, and the slow waxing and waning of subsequent generations of trees, the main appearance of the valley has altered little since Sir James's death 110 years ago. It still breaks upon the traveller's eye, as he comes southward from Maybole, green and fertile, 'gashed with glens and patched with plantations,' as pleasantly as, in Sir James's day, it broke upon the sentimental regard of the poet Hew Ainslie.[85] The age of the improvers was ended, and other men entered into their labours. The traveller who passes down Sir James's road, and looks across Sir Adam's fields at the silver-grey house set against the dark masses of his and Lord Kilkerran's woods, may well reflect that nowhere have utility and beauty been more charmingly blended.

> *Ille terrarum mihi praeter omnes*
> *Angulus ridet.*

Though what I have written here concerns only those who may be called the strategists of the new agriculture and silviculture, I do not forget those whose actual labours pushed on their experiments and brought their designs to fulfilment: factors, grieves, farmers, masons, joiners, hinds, foresters andlabourers of all kinds. But these belong to the great army 'which have no memorial' - save their own anonymous achievements. They left no diaries nor letters, and so as historical figures survive only by allusions and an occasional scrap of holograph writing.

We know the names of many. There was John Henry, Sir Adam's factor, who lived at Ladyburn (where I spent much of my childhood) and whose signature is almost as familiar to me as that of his employer - whom Henry served not only as factor but also as an obedient 'parchment baron' on the roll of Ayrshire voters. There was William Jackson, Sir Adam's tenant of Moorston, whose fields had 'every appearance of good husbandry, regularly conducted'.[86] There was James McMillan the ploughman Sir Adam employed, who in the late summer of 1775 'fell into a lingering distemper, which unfitted him for work, for very near two years - in all which time', John Henry recorded, 'he was maintained in the familly, having bed, board, and washing as usual' besides his full wages, and 'began to work in the year 1777, in harvest time, and has been very well ever since'. And there was 'old James Paterson at Crosshill', who, as my great-grandfather noted in his diary on 18 October 1842, was 'altogether making a beautiful job' of huilding 'the excellent dyke' at the head of the Lady Glen.

Coming down to the present century, there was, in my own childhood, Mungo McInnes, drainer since my grandfather's days, who knew every culvert and underground watercourse on the estate as a surgeon knows the sinews and nerves of the human body; and there is to-day David Andrew, estate joiner like his father before him, whose craftsmanship has contributed something to the fabric of almost every building on the property. One conspicuous monument of David's skill is a gate which, nearly thirty years ago, took a first prize at the Highland Show.

Many, many others since 'the lads' who worked on Lord Kilkerran's first improvements have suffered 'many a wet skin' in the draining and fencing, the planting and building, and lie now in the kirkyards of Dailly or Crosshill. If their names are lost, their work remains, in the enduring characters of dyke and wood, field and fence, written large across the landscape of to-day.

1 Of which the best documented is that of Monymusk, described in *Monymusk Papers* (1718-55), Scottish History Society, 1945, and *Life and Labour on an Aberdeenshire Estate*, 1735-50, Third Spalding Club, 1946, both edited by Dr Henry Hamilton.

2 *Monymusk Papers*, pp. 72-3.

3 *Memoirs of Sir John Clerk of Penicuik*, Scottish History Society, 1892, pp. 74, 99, 136.

4 '*Pascuis fecunda, nee infelix frumento.*'-Rerum Scoticarum Historia, ed. Robert Fribarn, 1727, p. 13.

5 *Archaeological and Historical Collections relating to the Counties of Ayr and Wigton*, vol. iv (1884), p. 17.

6 I can find this word in no dictionary but take it to mean 'glens'.

7 Quoted from Sir James Balfour's Collections in *The Historie of the Kennedyis*, ed. Robert Pitcairn, 1880, p. 187.

8 When the new parish church of Dailly, which he calls 'of late erected', was built.

9 "A Description of Carrict' in *Macfarlane's Geographical Collections*, Scot. Hist. Soc., vol. ii, 1907, pp. 10-12.

10 *A Journey Through Scotland*, 1723, p. 328.

11 Nisbet's *A System of Heraldry*, p. 411.

12 Paterson's *History of Ayrshire* (1863 ed.): *Kyle*, p. clviii.

13 Charles Rogers: *Boswelliana*, pp. 283-4; cp. a covert reference in *The Private Papers of James Boswell*, vol. xiii, p. 233.

14 Playfair's *Baronetage*, Appendix, pp. lxxiv-lxxv. My grandfather noted a tradition that the account of the Fergusson family in this work was 'written or revised by Lord Hermand', Sir Adam's younger brother. Some of it at least was written by Sir Adam himself, for a draft of certain passages is among his papers.

15 Playfair's *Baronetage* p. lxxv.

16 The name is on record as 'Ballemaklunican' as early as 1361 in the Cassillis Papers.

17 General Register of Sasines, vol. 70, No. 119.

18 Not in 1680, as stated by Playfair.

19 When a George Kennedy of Balmaclanachan is on record (Cassillis MSS).

20 *Macfarlane's Geographical Collections*, vol. ii, p.ll.

21 *Ibid*, p. 20.

22 Sir John Stirling Maxwell: *Shrines and Homes of Scotland*, 1937, p.191.

23 The local tradition was recorded by Sir Adam; also by his nephew Sir James from the recollections of Lord Hermand. Cp. Paterson's *History of Ayrshire: Kyle*, p. clix.

24 Alexander Nisbet: *A System of Heraldry*, p. 412.

25 Balfour's Collections quoted in *The Historie of the Kennedyis*, p.185.

26 See John Struthers: *The History of Scotland from the Union to 1748*, 1827-8, vol. i, p. xiii.

27 Paterson's *History of Ayrshire*: Carrick, p. 231.

28 Rev. George Turnbull, D.D.: *A South Ayrshire Parish*, 1908, p.91.

29 Jamieson quotes two instances of hag as meaning 'one cutting or felling of a certain quantity of copse wood'; and Cockburn of Ormistoun often uses the word in this sense.

30 *Macfarlane's Geographical Collections*, vol. ii, p. 11.

31 According to the *Gentleman's Magazine* for that month, though the *Return of Members of Parliament* gives the date of his election as May 30.

32 J. D. Humphreys: *Correspondence and Diary of Philip Doddridge, D.D.*, vol. iv, p. 285.

33 Fergusson to Hugh, third Earl of Loudoun, 5 March 1730 (Loudoun MSS).

34 G. W. T. Omond: *The Lord Advocates of Scotland*, 1883, vol. i, p.345.

35 James Fergusson: *John Fergusson (1727-50)*, 1948, pp. 45-6, 48-9.

36 Robert Maxwell: *Select Transactions of the Honourable the Society of Improvers*, 1743, pp.19-20.

37 *A Treatise concerning the Manner of Fallowing of Ground*, 1724, pp. 7-8. The anonymous author was William Macintosh of Borlum.

38 *Scotland and Scotsmen in the Eighteenth Century*, ed. Alexander Allardyce, 1888, vol. ii, p. 226.

39 *Letters of John Cockburn of Ormistoun to his Gardener*, Scottish History Society, 1904, pp. xxiv, 91-2.

40 [Eighth] Duke of Argyll: *Scotland as It Was and as It Is*, second ed., 1887, pp. 255-6.

41 *Monymusk Papers*, 1713-55, p.lxx.

42 H. G. Graham: *The Social Life of Scotland in the Eighteenth Century*, 1928 ed., p. 68.

43 H. G. Graham: *Literary and Historical Essays*. 1908, p. 156.

44 A. F. Tytler: *Life of Lord Kames*, vol. i, p. 36.

45 *Ibid.*

46 *John Fergusson, 1727-50*, p. 59.

47 James Fergusson: *Letters of George Dempster to Sir Adam Fergusson (1756-1813)*, 1934, reprinted 2004, pp. 18, 23.

48 Lord Auchinleck to John, fourth Earl of Loudoun, 29 June 1754 and 26 September 1755 (Loudoun MSS).

49 *Registrum de Panmure*, vol. i, p. lxxxvi.

50 National Library of Scotland MS 2968 (Culloden MSS), f.126.

51 *Diary of George Ridpath*, Scottish History Society, 1922, p. 226.

52 Lord Cockburn: *Memorials of His Time*, 1856, p. 82.

53 *The Author's Earnest Cry and Prayer to. ... the Scotch Representatives in the House of Commons.*

54 Diary of Peggy Hope, afterwards Mrs Thomas Thomson, from a transcript by Dr Thomas Lauder Thomson (MS in the possession of Mr George Burnett, Old Parsonage, Calderbridge, Cumberland, to whom I am indebted for permission to quote it).

55 *Ex inform.* Professor Frederick A. Pottle.

56 I owe the discovery of this letter to Dr L, W. Sharp, the librarian of the University of Edinburgh. It is not recorded in Professor Pottle's *The Literary Career of James Boswell.*

57 *Letters of George Dempster to Sir Adam Fergusson*, p. 172.

58 It was not, as often stated, his better known contemporary Dr Adam Ferguson, the philosopher, who was in this group. See Dr Hugh Blair's letter to Henry Mackenzie, 20 December 1797, in the *Report of the Committee of the Highland Society on the Authenticity of the Poems of Ossian*, 1805, Appendix, p. 58.

59 See my article 'An Erse Poem' in *An Gaidheal* for February and March, 1938.

60 James Coutts: *A History of the University of Glasgow*, 1909, p. 335.

61 *Scottish Historical Review*, vol. xxvi, pp.128-30.

62 *The Private Papers of James Boswell*, vol. x, p. 29.

63 The 'coalheugh of Yellowlee' is mentioned in the Cassillis MSS in a charter of 1566. But according to the Rev. C. H. Dick (*Highways and Byways in Galloway and Carrick*, 1916, p. 385) 'there is evidence of coal having been wrought in this district so long ago as 1415'.

64 The date is given categorically by Mr Dick (*op. cit.*, p. 386) but may be only derived from the phrase 'about 45 years ago' in the *Statistical Account of Scotland* (Kirkoswald), vol. x, p. 497, published in 1794.

65 *The Private Papers of James Boswell*, vol. xiii, p. 233.

66 *Statistical Account of Scotland* (Dailly), vol. x, p. 43. The Scots acre is 6150.4 sq. yds. as opposed to the English acre of 4840 sq. yds. '400 Scots acres' is therefore over 508 English acres.

67 The father (by his second wife) of two remarkable sons, Thomas Thomson the antiquary and John Thomson ('of Duddingston') the landscape painter, both of whom were born in the manse of Dailly.

68 Andrew Wight: *Recent State of Husbandry in Scotland*, 1778, vol. iii, p. 156.

69 Colonel Fullarton's *Report on Ayrshire* to the Board of Agriculture, 1793, pp. 41-2.

70 Wight, *op. cit.*, pp. 157-64.

71 *A Treatise of Agriculture*, 1762, p. 101, note. The anonymous author was Adam Dickson.

72 *Statistical Account of Scotland* (Kirkoswald), vol. x, p. 487.

73 *Statistical Account of Scotland* (Dailly), pp. 43-4, 51, note.

74 *Ibid.* (Kilmaurs), vol. ix, p. 357.

75 But he had told Henry Dundas in 1777, during 'the coal cause' against the tenth Lord Cassillis, that 'of the three places of the hill in question, in one there is no coal of any value to work; in another it is impossible to subsist for heat; and in the third, I think, there is not above one acre of coal. . . a matter certainly of very small value'.

76 Born 1700, served heir to his father 1704, and died 1759.

77 Sir Hew Dalrymple, fourth baronet of North Berwick, took the name and arms of Hamilton on succeeding his uncle in the estate of Bargany, which marched with Kilkerran. This was his son, Sir Hew Dalrymple Hamilton (1774-1834), who had been M.P. for Ayrshire 1803-6. He and James Fergusson had married sisters (daughters of Admiral Duncan), so that there would be 'little difficulty' in getting this concession from one who was both a neighbour and a near connection.

78 *Letters of George Dempster to Sir Adam Fergusson*, p. 394.

79 *Scots Magazine*, vol. lxxv, p. 879.

80 Paterson's *History of Ayrshire (Carrick)*, p. 210.

81 He was no relation to the Kilkerran family.

82 James Fergusson of Crosshill to Thomas Kennedy of Dunure, 15 November 1798 (Dunure MSS, in the possession of Lt.-Col. J. K. MacFarlan of Dunure).

83 *New Statistical Account of Scotland* (Dailly), vol. v, p. 387.

84 *Letters on the Affairs of Scotland*, 1874, p. 220.

85 Hew Ainslie: *A Pilgrimage to the Land of Burns*, 1892 ed., p. 98.

86 Wight, *op cit.*, vol. iii, p. 156.

3

The Queen in Ayrshire

On Tuesday, 3 July 1956, Queen Elizabeth II, accompanied by the Duke of Edinburgh, paid an official visit to Ayrshire. 'Visit' is the rather inept word habitually used nowadays when the Sovereign appears anywhere outside her capital, even when she is in residence at the Palace of Holyroodhouse which has been the home of her family for many generations longer than Buckingham Palace. In former times an official journey by a reigning monarch through one part or another of the kingdom was known as a 'progress'. Its purpose might be to dispense justice or to suppress rebellion; it was more often to change residence from one palace or castle to another, and at the same time to consume such of the royal revenues as were rendered in the form of food and drink; and it was sometimes to escape from the insanitary conditions of a city or to remove to a safe distance from another outbreak of 'the pest'.

But the modern monarchs of Great Britain, who have been more truly the servants of their people than almost any of their predecessors, make progresses for other reasons: to inspect and encourage new enterprises in industry, agriculture, engineering, social services, and occasionally the arts; to familiarize themselves with provinces of their realm to which official duties have not as yet taken them; and to allow their subjects the actual sight of themselves for which no picture, even though modern science can make it both move and speak, can ever be an altogether acceptable substitute.

Queen Victoria began this modern style of progress. King George V and King George VI continued and extended it. Queen Elizabeth II has done the same, and has moreover visited far corners of her kingdom to which few and in some cases none of her royal ancestors ever penetrated.

The Queen's progress through Ayrshire, long hoped for and eagerly awaited by its people, was all too brief, lasting some nine hours of a single summer day. It embraced, naturally, the more populous parts of the county, the industrialized districts of Cunningham and Kyle; and she passed through only the northern fringe of the ancient earldom of Carrick, the home of her ancestor King Robert Bruce and the hereditary appanage of her son the young Duke of Rothesay (not yet created Prince of Wales). But it was a well-filled day, during which Her Majesty managed to visit and receive the official greetings of most of the burghs of Ayrshire. There was some dry complaint that she saw 'nothing but provosts and pitheads', and indeed she could see little of the county's rural scenery, the winding, wooded valleys, the broad pastures, the great hills ribbed with drystane dykes that sweep away to the east and south - the essential Ayrshire which centuries of history have hardly changed. But she did in her crowded hours see more of the county and its people than did the last sovereign to make an official progress through Ayrshire, nearly four hundred years before hers.

In the long interval between there had been, it is true, a few brief visits by royal personages, but they were not progresses. During the Second World War, King George VI, under the conditions of secrecy necessary at that time, inspected some of his troops who were being trained in Ayrshire, and some years earlier, while he was still Duke of York, laid the foundation stone of the new County Buildings in Ayr. King Edward VIII, as Prince of Wales, once spent part of a November day in Ayrshire, out with the Eglinton Hunt. But though Queen Victoria was once off the coast in the royal yacht she never visited the county; neither did the son and grandson who succeeded her.

Of the House of Hanover, George IV was the only sovereign who set foot in Scotland at all, and he was never outside the Lothians. Before him there is a long gap back to Charles II's reign. His brother James, Duke of York and Albany, afterwards King James VII, held state for a few months in Edinburgh as the King's Commissioner to the Parliament of Scotland in 1680-1, but he was never in Ayrshire; and the King's own brief and troubled residence in his northern kingdom in 1650 and 1651 had included no visit to the south-west. Charles I, born in Dunfermline, left Scotland as a boy, and after his succession to the English and Scottish Crowns visited it only in 1633 for his coronation and in 1641, and was never nearer to Ayr than Linlithgow. His father James VI in 1598 proposed to take ship from Ayr to Kintyre on an expedition to restore order among his turbulent subjects in the West Highlands. But though 'his majesteis progres to Kintyre' led him to spend a few days at the castle of Sorn on the River Ayr he apparently went no further west[1], and his expedition petered out.

And so, searching backwards, we come to the year 1563 and the month of August, when Mary, Queen of Scots, made her progress through Ayrshire and spent not one day but ten among her Ayrshire subjects. This was the last royal progress through the county till that of her descendant in the thirteenth degree, Queen Elizabeth II, in 1956.

Queen Mary's progress followed a period which by the standards of her reign had been fairly peaceful but had not been without some anxieties. Huntly's rebellion of the previous year had been officially concluded, so to speak, by the formal forfeiture on 28 May of Huntly himself (already dead) and Sutherland. Parliament had met, for the first time since the Queen's return to Scotland two years before. The burghs had complained bitterly to it of the heavy import duties levied by the Danes, which were crippling the Scottish Baltic trade, and an embassy to the King of Denmark on the subject had been despatched and returned without effect. The matter of the Queen's second marriage, not to be resolved till she wedded her cousin Lord Darnley two years later, had been agitating not only the courts of England and Spain but Edinburgh itself. The notion of the Queen's marrying a Spanish prince, which it had become known that she was entertaining, was highly unpopular in Scotland. Before Parliament rose on 6 June, John Knox, in a sermon preached 'before the most part of the nobility', had spoken out with characteristic bluntness against any marriage of the Queen of Scots to 'an infidel - and all Papists', he added, 'are infidels'. Summoned to the presence of his indignant sovereign, he had reduced her, by his own account, to an 'inordinate passion' of tears[2].

Not unnaturally the Queen, who was not yet 21 years old, chose to make her summer progress through the territories of nobles friendly and loyal to her and not likely to plague her with unwelcome advice or to insult her religion: the Earls of Argyll, Eglinton, and Cassillis, the Master of Maxwell (afterwards Lord Herries), and Lord Somerville. Her route took her through a wide quarter of her realm which she had never yet viewed.

It made a great circle through the west and south-west, by Stirlingshire, Glasgow, and Dunbartonshire into Argyll, thence through Ayrshire and Galloway into Dumfriesshire, and back to Craigmillar near Edinburgh by way of Crawfordjohn, Peebles, Borthwick, Dalhousie, and Roslin.

Buchanan's statement that 'the rest of the summer the Queen gave up to hunting in Atholl' is either sheer invention or a confusion with the great hunt in Atholl that she witnessed the following year[3]. The journey was indeed something of a holiday tour, but not altogether. The Registers of the Great Seal and Privy Seal show that the Queen transacted a certain amount of official business during her travels, even at places so remote from her capital as Inveraray and St. Mary's Isle; and she held a meeting of her Privy Council in Glasgow on 8 July and another in Dumfries on 20 August, the last being to consider the reply to a letter of 19 August from the English Warden of the Middle Marches, written from Carlisle[4]. But her progress through Ayrshire had nothing to interrupt whatever pleasure it gave her.

She travelled almost wholly along the coast, scarcely ever out of sight of the sea. There were no more roads in that region than anywhere else at that time, but there were bridges over the rivers of Irvine, Ayr, Doon, and Girvan near their mouths; and there were several places, at convenient distances apart, fit for lodging a Queen and her train. The cool breezes off the sea would make riding over the short, springy turf pleasant in the August days. Besides, the country inland, especially in Carrick, was thickly wooded, and in many places boggy, with numerous waters to be crossed.

We do not know exactly who accompanied the Queen, nor, since the Lord Treasurer's accounts for the year 1563 have not survived, have we any details of her clothes and baggage. She travelled, at any rate, with only a small attendance, for their transport consisted of but eighteen horses and six baggage mules. This we know from the stabling accounts kept by her French equerry[5], who recorded where she spent each day and night and the costs of lodging the animals. But the royal party must have often included a fluid following of local notables. At Irvine and Ayr the magistrates would meet the Queen at their burgh boundaries and escort her until she left them; and the several nobles who were her hosts would accompany her, each through his own lands. The local barons, lairds, and gentlemen, too, would ride intermittently in the Queen's train, perhaps to show their loyalty, perhaps hoping for favours, perhaps just to see and be seen, each with his little knot of attendant kinsmen and servants trailing respectfully in the rear. There would be Montgomeries and Cunninghams, Boyles and Mures, in the north; Craufurds, Campbells, and Wallaces in Kyle; and throughout Carrick a preponderance of Kennedys, with Fergussons, Boyds, Cathcarts, and more Mures and Craufurds.

The tall young Queen, who loved riding and gaiety, must have been the centre all the way of a cheerful and carefree company. There was apparently no public business to be considered on this part of her journey; and in those days sovereigns seldom had to go out of their way to display themselves to their subjects - who were none the less at perfect liberty to come and watch them pass by. No doubt there were cheers and blessings and waving bonnets. But there must have been also some dark looks and surly mutterings in the background. The Queen had many, perhaps a majority of Papists in her train; and, as Knox recorded disapprovingly, she 'had her mass' at each house where she stayed. Knox had preached in Kyle the previous autumn, and George Hay at the same time 'with great fruit in all the churches of Carrick'[6]. Under the influence of these powerful preachers, seventy-eight Ayrshire noblemen, barons, and lairds had signed a covenant in Ayr on 4 September to maintain the preaching of the Gospel and the ministry, and to assist 'the hoill body of the Protestantis within this realme'[7]. These eminent men and those whom they represented must have balanced their pleasure at the sight of their young Queen with suspicions of the policy she was pursuing: well justified too, since earlier this year she had been writing to the Pope that she would do all in her power to make her subjects obey the decrees of the Council of Trent, 'if God, by his grace, is able to reduce and destroy the heresies'.

Whatever enthusiasm, therefore, was shown by the people in Irvine, Ayr, and elsewhere where the Queen passed was probably not quite whole-hearted. The attendant throng of gentlemen, too, can have been by no means always in harmony, and some groups would be avoiding each other for other than religious reasons. There was no love lost, for instance, between the Montgomeries and the Cunninghams; and in Carrick there was 'deidlie feid and inimitie' between the Kennedys who adhered to the Earl of Cassillis and the Craufurds of Camlarg, on account of 'the hurting and wounding' a few months before of one 'Hary Kennedy *alias* Mady'[8]. The Craufurds also had a smouldering dispute of many years' standing with the Fergussons of Kilkerran, which broke out into open and scandalous violence less than a year after the Queen's progress[9]. Further south still, Adam Boyd of Penkill cannot have been on speaking terms with James Eccles of that ilk, the laird of Kildonan, who had failed to pay his rent for the year 1562 for his tenancy of Boyd's lands of Trochraig and had also refused to remove from them at last Whitsunday though lawfully warned to do so. The two were at this time pursuing each other by action and counter-action in the Court of Session[10].

The Queen slept for her first night in Ayrshire, 31 July, at Lord Sempill's castle of Southannan, for she had crossed the Firth of Clyde that day from Dunoon after her journey through Argyll. Lord Sempill, an elderly man, was a Roman Catholic. His illegitimate son John later married one of the Queen's Maries, Mary Livingstone: perhaps this was the occasion when the couple first met.

Only a few stones are left of Southannan, and there is no trace today of the Eglinton Castle where the Queen spent her next night in Ayrshire, 1 August. Here she was the Earl of Eglinton's guest, and the stabling of her horses and mules cost, as the equerry noted, '*neant*' (nothing). Eglinton, some 30 years of age, was an old acquaintance, for he had been one of the nobles who had gone over to France in 1561 to escort the Queen back to her own country. She stayed with him till after dinner on 2 August, and in the afternoon rode south through Irvine, and reached Ayr in time for supper. There is nothing to confirm the tradition in Irvine that she stayed in the Seagate Castle there. She certainly spent no night in the town, and the local historian thinks it unlikely that the building itself was erected till a year or two after her progress[11].

It was an easy ride to Ayr, through almost flat country. Over the Auld Brig and by the High Street, the Queen entered the old burgh where she was to stay for two nights. Nothing of the 'Auld Ayr' she saw remains today but the tower of St. John's Church, the bridge, and 'the Sheriff's lodging' - the town house of Sir Matthew Campbell of Loudoun, hereditary Sheriff of Ayr, known today as Loudoun Hall and recently restored to something of its original appearance. As the extant burgh accounts have a gap at this date, we do not know how Ayr received the Queen. Certainly there would be a 'propine' of wine and sweetmeats offered by the magistrates at the least. There is no record of where the Queen and her train stayed. Sir Herbert Maxwell conjectured that it was in the monastery of St. John - but no such monastery ever existed. Their lodgings were probably in private houses, and were possibly hired, for the Queen's equerry had to pay for oats and straw for the horses and mules, just over £19. But the Sheriff may have had the honour of lodging the Queen herself.

After dinner on 4 August the Queen passed on to Dunure. When over the Doon, crossing by the high single-arched bridge that still stands, she was in the Earl of Cassillis's territory - 'a barrant cuntree but for bestiall' an English spy reported contemptuously about this time, adding, not very accurately, 'The people for the moste part speketht Erishe' [12].

At Dunure ('a fare castell, not stronge nor worthy fortifying', thought the Englishman), the Queen remained for three nights, her longest stay in Ayrshire. Cassillis, her host, 'that young papist erle', was only a few months older than she, and perhaps took her out hawking at grouse, partridges, and hares on the green hillsides overlooking the firth with their splendid view of silver sea and blue islands backed by the three pointed peaks of Arran and the far grey outline of Kintyre. Some visitors she certainly received here. Among them may have been Cassillis's uncle, the pious and earnest Abbot Quintin Kennedy of Crossraguel, a devoted champion of the Roman Church who the previous year had challenged John Knox to dispute with him on the Scriptural justification of the Mass, and held his own during three days of argument in Maybole. He still lived in his abbey, a bare six miles distant from Dunure. Other visitors probably included some of Cassillis's principal clansmen such as Thomas Kennedy of Bargany, who was to be the Queen's host later, and John Kennedy of Blairquhan. 'These tuo,' the English spy reported, 'be nothing inferior in leving to therle of Cassills'; and there were other Kennedy lairds also who would have felt themselves slighted if their young chief had not presented them to the Queen.

One small gathering of local lairds, at least, there must have been at Dunure during the Queen's stay there. While in Ayrshire she issued two precepts under her Privy Seal; the first at Southannan, the second at Dunure. The latter (wrongly dated in the Register 15 August, by which day the Queen was in Wigtownshire) was for a charter to Robert Wallace, son and apparent heir of Hew Wallace of Carnell, granting him some lands in Kyle-Stewart. These lands had been held previously by two Kennedy sisters, Gelis Kennedy, widow of John Grierson of Lag, and Jonet Kennedy, wife of George Kennedy of Barclanachan, who resigned them in Robert's favour [13]. The formal ceremony of resignation 'by staff and baston' into the superior's hands was usually performed to a deputy when the superior was the sovereign or a great noble. But in this case the record shows that the resignation was made *apud Dunnure*, and *in manibus S.D.N. regine*: the opportunity was taken to enact this little ceremony, symbolic of feudal duty, to the Sovereign in person. Kyle-Stewart, like Carrick, is an appanage of the Prince and Steward of Scotland, who is also Duke of Rothesay and Earl of Carrick, and the Queen, having as yet no heir, was acting *tanquam Princeps* and at this moment resident in the Stewartry lands; so the moment was felicitously chosen. The resignation was actually performed on the ladies' behalf by procurators, who were probably local lairds, and it may be assumed that several Kennedys and Wallaces were present [14].

Dunure, though not thought 'worthy fortifying', perhaps because at that date it possessed no harbour, was superbly sited on a high rocky headland overlooking the firth and a wide stretch of shore, and the view as well as the company may have tempted Queen Mary to linger there. But on 7 August she continued her journey, after dinner was over, along the coast to Ardmillan, a ride of something over twenty miles. The high rectangular tower of Ardmillan was snugly tucked under a steep hill facing the sea, a short distance beyond the Water of Girvan's mouth, and here the Queen's host was 'the Gudeman of Ardmillan', John Kennedy, a middle-aged cousin of the laird of Bargany. Ardmillan is the only one of the Ayrshire houses where Queen Mary stayed which is today still standing and inhabited, though much altered. Here the equerry again entered *Neant* in his accounts, as he had done at Dunure and was to do again at Ardstinchar, the spacious and lofty castle of Thomas Kennedy of Bargany. This lay a short day's ride farther on, over the height of Bennan Head, with the steep rocky island of Ailsa Craig in full view most of the way.

Ardstinchar, like Dunure, stood high on a precipitous foundation, though not quite so near the sea, overlooking the mouth of the Water of Stinchar. Here the Queen stayed only one night, though her lodging was probably not inferior to what she had enjoyed at Dunure. The company may have been a shade less congenial, the welcome loyal rather than enthusiastic, more formal than friendly. Thomas Kennedy of Bargany was an elderly man and at this time possibly a sick one, for he died the following year[15]. The Queen's active host was probably his son and heir, another Thomas, who, though he won the reputation of being wise and courteous, as well as 'passing kynd'[16], was possibly a little stiff in his behaviour to the Queen. Though married for the past seven years to Lord Eglinton's sister, he did not, like Eglinton, hold by the old church. On the contrary he was an ardent Reformer, and his signature, as 'Bargany younger', had been one of the twenty-seven appended to Knox's 'Book of Discipline' in January 1561[17]. Though he was willing to regard Lord Cassillis as 'his cheif'[18], his father had been at pains to make it quite clear that the family were not the Earl's vassals[19]; and both of them would receive the Queen as loyal subjects but in no sense as Cassillis's dependents.

Everywhere during the Queen's progress, the equerry had difficulties, when writing up his accounts, with the local names. Ayr he had rendered 'Era' and Dunure 'Duneura'; and Ardmillan, which he made into 'Ermelan', had almost defeated him. 'Arstinchel', however, was not a bad effort for Ardstinchar, better at least than 'Glainleux', which was his version of Glenluce, the abbey in Wigtownshire to which the Queen and her train rode on next day after dinner. After riding down Glenapp, Queen Mary passed out of Ayrshire, which she was never to enter again. There is no contemporary report of what impression she made on those who there entertained her, heard her speak and laugh, or merely watched her ride past. But some evidence that she left them a lasting and happy memory seems to lie in the striking number of Ayrshiremen who five years later rallied to her standard after she had escaped from Lochleven, and fought for her at the battle of Langside. The French ambassador, who 'rode to Hamilton to the Queen, and dealt between the parties for peace, but was not heard', told Sir James Melville, 'that he never did see so many men so suddenly convened'[20]; and the number of Ayrshiremen among them, mustered from a county where the Queen's supporters might be thought to have been but a small minority, can be deduced from the long tale of those recorded as having forfeited lands and goods in punishment for their loyalty[21]. Most of them, however, gained remissions later on.

Bargany and his brother Hew Kennedy of Bennan fought for the Regent in that brief but decisive battle, as might have been expected; and Lord Sempill had turned against Queen Mary after Darnley's murder. But in the Queen's army were Lord Cassillis and his brother Thomas; Lord Eglinton, Lord Boyd with two of his sons and many of his name, and Sir Matthew Campbell of Loudoun, Sheriff of Ayr; also Hew Craufurd of Kilbirnie and his son William, David Barclay of Ladyland, John Boswell of Auchinleck, William Barclay of Perceton, William Stewart of Dunduff, John Schaw of Grimmet, George Nesbitt of Templeland, and the laird of Penkill's son, Mr. James Boyd of Trochraig. Another who suffered escheat with these was George Kennedy of Barclanachan, who with his wife had probably kissed the Queen's hand when she stayed at Dunure. More remarkable is the escheat of George Corrie of Kelwood; for although a neighbour and dependent of the Earl of Cassillis he himself was an avowed and consistent Reformer. Like young Bargany, he had subscribed the Book of Discipline; and he had also signed the Ayr Covenant of 1562 and the Bond of Association against Popery of 1567. Perhaps he was one who fell under the Queen's spell while she was at Dunure, and remembered it nearly five years afterwards.

Besides these, there are recorded the names of several men of humbler rank, like Nevin McCully in Aird, John Broun in Lane, and Gilbert Macilwraith in Trolorg, of whom nothing else is known but that they had made themselves culpably conspicuous at Langside. There must have been many others who managed to elude notice there or afterwards. It was not a slaughterous battle, for 'there were not many horsemen to pursue after them, and the Regent cried to save and not to kill; and Grange was never cruel, so that there were but few slain and taken'[22]. Besides, the two forces contained kinsmen, friends, and neighbours unwillingly arrayed against each other. The dead on both sides, according to one account, 'exceidit not the nomber of tua hundreth'[23]. Among the prisoners taken by the Regent's party were the Master of Cassillis, brother to the Earl, and the Sheriff, Sir Matthew Campbell. Eglinton hid himself in a house under straw until nightfall and then escaped[24]. He had been one of the first noblemen to rally to the Queen's standard after her escape from

Lochleven, and was one of the last to yield to the inevitable and make his peace with the new government. Another faithful supporter was Cassillis, who for several years remained loyal to the Queen's hopeless cause and received many letters from her in her English prisons, signed 'Your guid freind, MARIE R.'

As she signed those letters, Queen Mary must often have thought of her early years in Scotland, and of a good horse, and a fresh salt wind, and the sun on the sea, and the fair castle of Dunure.

1 Treasurer's Accounts (unprinted), 1597-8, ff. 87-93.

2 John Knox's *History of the Reformation in Scotland*, ed. Dickinson, ii, pp. 80-4.

3 W. A. Gatherer, *The Tyrannous Reign of Mary Stewart (George Buchanan's Account)*, p. 80.

4 *Privy Council Register*, i, pp. 241, 243-4.

5 In H.M. General Register House: partly printed, edited by Sir Herbert Maxwell, in *Scottish Historical Review*, xviii, pp. 5-7.

6 Knox, *ut cit.*, ii, p. 55.

7 James King Hewison, *The Covenanters*, i, pp. 54-5.

8 Acts and Decreets,xxx, ff. 358-9.

9 Pitcairn's *Criminal Trials in Scotland*, i, pp. 456-8; *Calendar of Scottish Papers*, ii, p. 76.

10 Acts and Decreets, xxv, ff. 118-19; xxvi, ff. 241-2; xxvii, f. 274; xxviii, ff. 145-6, 266, 400

11 A. F. McJannet, *Royal Burgh of Irvine*, p. 99.

12 *Archaeological and Historical Collections relating to Ayr and Wigton*, iv, pp. 17-19.

13 They were sisters and heirs of umquhile John Kennedy of Culzean (Acts and Decreets, xxiv, f. 136).

14 *R.S.S.*, v, 1439.

15 In June 1564 (Edinburgh Testaments, vii, ff. 374-6).

16 *Historie of the Kennedyis*, p. 25.

17 Knox, *ut cit.*, ii, p. 324.

18 Acts and Decreets, xxxviii, ff. 182-4.

19 Transumpt (22 March 1623) of instrument of 8 October 1557 in Bargany MSS (Ardstinchar writs).

20 Sir James Melville, *Memoirs of his own Life*, ed. W. Mackay Mackenzie (Abbey Classics), p. 100.

21 Register of the Privy Seal (unprinted), vols. xxxvii, xxxviii.

22 Melville, *op. cit.*, p. 102.

23 *Historie of King James the Sext*, p. 26.

24 *Calendar of Scottish Papers*, ii, pp. 405, 407.

5. Crossraguel Abbey

6. Trochrague

7. Crosshill, built on land feued from
Kirkbride and Kilkerran

8. William Niven's house in Maybole

4

The Last Monks of Crossraguel

There is hardly a monastery in Scotland the ruins of which remain as entire as those of Crossraguel, a daughter house of the Cluniac abbey of Paisley, which was founded by Duncan, 1st Earl of Carrick, in the time of Alexander II. It lies in a sheltered hollow in the heart of Carrick, about a mile from Maybole, in a countryside that has changed little since the eighteenth century though a good deal since the Middle Ages when the new abbey was surrounded by extensive woods. The abbey church itself, the abbot's house, the cloister with its central well, the quarters of the brethren and the capacious storehouses testifying to the productivity of their wide lands, all survive almost complete although roofless; and the tall gate-house and the chapter-house and sacristy with their simple but handsome vaulted roofs are virtually whole. I have known and loved Crossraguel since childhood, from even before the time when the Ministry of Works brought its ruins to their present secure and charming order, and it gives me pleasure to recall that their survival owes much to the care bestowed on them by more than one generation of my family while they owned the surrounding farms. Sir Adam Fergusson of Kilkerran, a cultivated and scholarly man, took care that his agricultural improvements should bring no harm to the abbey. 'This ruin,' it was written in 1794. 'is preserved with great care and attention, the tenants not being allowed to take down and use any stone from the abbey itself.'[1]

Two generations later, in my great-grandfather's time, 'the ruins were thoroughly examined and made secure';[2] and my grandfather had the belfry gable repaired and pointed when 'the next severe gale would assuredly have thrown it down'[3] It was an uncle of my mother's, too, who edited the publication of the abbey's muniments.[4]

It is not difficult, when walking among the ruins on a quiet summer day, listening to the bees murmuring among the wallflowers and the ripple of the burn that once turned the Abbey's mill and supplied its buildings with water, to imagine the peaceful yet active life which its community of Cluniac monks once led. They were in every way a reputable little body. No scandals, even in the years immediately preceding the Reformation, attached to the brethren of Crossraguel; and indeed in 1515 they were formally exempted from a disciplinary visitation of all the other monasteries in Scotland ordered by the Pope, a fact which, as the abbey's historian remarks, speaks volumes for the good order in which their late abbots had maintained them. All the more therefore does the question suggest itself of what happened to them when the Reformation arrived and in the next few years the Crown stripped the monasteries of their great estates and bestowed them on laymen.

It is seldom realized that in Scotland the religious communities were much less harshly treated at the Reformation than in England. In Scotland there was no 'dissolution' of the monasteries. A few monks joined the clergy of the Reformed Church, such as William Kirkpatrick, a monk of Kilwinning who became the first post-Reformation minister of that parish, and John Sanderson, a monk of Glenluce who became 'reader' there, but none seems to have done so from the small group at Crossraguel. It was difficult for monks to change their way of life, and most of them probably preferred to continue their quiet lives in the quarters to which they had been so long accustomed.[5] A few no doubt drifted away into secular employments, and some married. But for those who wished to remain where they were there was, as will be explained, at least no financial obstacle.

For the ruination or disappearance of many of our finest medieval churches the Reformers or the mobs they inflamed generally get the blame which properly belongs elsewhere: either to the Roman Church which had neglected their upkeep, the English who destroyed them in war, or subsequent heritors or local authorities who did not trouble or could not afford to maintain the buildings they had inherited. Actual violent destruction at the Reformation was mostly limited to the friaries. Many monasteries often suffered no damage at all, and their destruction was effected by some later generation for reasons quite other than religious. An example is the abbey of Deer of which Sir Robert Gordon of Straloch wrote, well on in the seventeenth century and recollecting the last years of the sixteenth, 'In my early youth I saw the church, the house, the monks' cells, the pleasant gardens and other things almost intact; but now the very stones have been taken away, and the plough is triumphant.' [6]

The Reformers of the West are recorded by Knox to have 'cast down' the friary of Failford and the abbeys of Kilwinning and Crossraguel.[7] But whatever was done at Failford, the abbey of Kilwinning served as the parish church for the next two centuries, and neglect and decay did not cause its great tower to fall till 1814. At Crossraguel there was probably no more than a formal 'purging' of the church itself, such as the destruction of most of the carved images and of those 'relics of the choir' which had been formally handed over to the last abbot at his consecration in 1548.[8] All evidence suggests that the monastic buildings and the church fabric were left untouched - to this day part of the high altar in the church still stands, an almost unique survival. The last abbot, Quintin Kennedy, who died in 1564, was the uncle of the Earl of Cassillis who, as has already been told, remained a Roman Catholic, and Kennedy authority would have been enough to restrain any intruders from more than the minimum of 'casting down'. After Abbot Quintin's death the abbot's house, a high four-storeyed erection to the south-east, the newest of all the abbey buildings, became the residence of the successive 'commendators' to whom the abbey lands were granted; and in the monks' quarters the former brethren remained to live out their blameless days unmolested.

They were very few. The community at Crossraguel had probably seldom numbered more than a dozen, and at the time of the Reformation it was even smaller. There were only eight monks when Abbot Kennedy was installed, and only nine in 1560, or ten if the abbot himself is included - the same number as there had been as long ago as 1405.[9] Here are their names: Dean John Mure, the sub-prior, Dean Robert McEwen, Dean Michael Dewar, Dean John Mure younger, Dean Nevin McEwen, Dean Gilbert McBurne, Dean Adam Maxwell, Dean Gilbert Kennedy, and Dean John Bryce. It was the two youngest of these, Gilbert Kennedy and John Bryce, who survived into the following century.

The historian of Crossraguel, Mr. F. C. Hunter Blair, points to evidence among the abbey charters that there were monks still living in the abbey in 1592 - 'a later period, probably, than in any monastery in

Scotland'.[10] But evidence which was unknown to him allows us to pursue their story for several years beyond even that date.

In their earliest zeal the Reformers had considered condemning monks to live on charity. The first General Assembly of the reformed Church of Scotland had sweepingly ordained that all who had been 'in the ministrie of the Popes kirk' should 'live upon the almes of the Kirk with the number of poore'.[11] But a little later it was settled that the monks should be entitled as before to receive their 'portions' in provisions and sometimes cash also, to be paid to them by those who now enjoyed the revenues of the former monastic lands. The monks were also to be allowed to continue occupying their 'chambers' and their 'yards' or gardens in the monastery's precincts, and that the Crossraguel monks did so is proved by a reference to 'the pur men that hes the yardis' at 'the place of Corsragall' in 1589. [12]

This provision for the monks' maintenance does not seem to have rested on any Act of Parliament. But by 1569 the payment of 'monks' portions' could be described as 'the common practick of the realme', and it was upheld on divers occasions by both the Privy Council and the Court of Session. It is the continuance of this 'practick' that enables us to trace something of the history of the last monks of Crossraguel.

By 1569 there were only six monks left in the community, by 1575 only five, and it might well be thought that it must soon be quite extinguished. But in 1597 we find evidence of two monks still surviving, thirty-seven years after the Reformation. The evidence is such as to make very clear the position and the rights of these two brethren. The 4th Earl of Cassillis, who had become the virtual owner of most of the former abbey lands, had undertaken to pay the surviving monks their 'portionis of victuall and silver usit and wont', and had apparently faithfully done so as long as he lived. At his death in 1576 he was succeeded by a minor, his son Gilbert, 5th Earl of Cassillis, afterwards one of the principal figures in the great Carrick vendetta between the families of Cassillis and Bargany, during whose minority the Cassillis estates were administered by his uncle Sir Thomas Kennedy of Culzean, known during that time as the Tutor of Cassillis. In his twenties Cassillis spent some time in France. He was in Paris in April 1596, [13] in London, presumably on his way back to Scotland, on I May 1597, [14] and came home late in July of that year. [15] On 7 October he signed at Maybole, with his uncle Culzean as one of the witnesses, a bond promising to pay Dean Gilbert Kennedy and Dean John Bryce their portions as undertaken by the late Earl for the years 1595 and 1596 (when they must have lapsed) 'and all utheris yeiris and termes to cum during thair lyftymes'. The bond stated three reasons for this undertaking. The two monks were said to have done the grantor 'diverss gratitudis and guid deidis'; he was obliged as heir to his father; and he was also obliged as heritable bailie of the regality of Crossraguel 'to sie the convent payit and assurit of thair saidis portionis yeirly'. [16]

But Cassillis did not fulfil his bond, either because of his financial embarrassments, which were considerable in 1599, or because of his absorption in his quarrel with the laird of Bargany. In 1602 Dean John Bryce raised an action against him, complaining that he had never been paid his 'usit portioun' at all, not merely from 1597 but since 1576, the year of the late Earl's death. Cassillis behaved in rather a shabby manner in resisting this claim on the ground that it did not state precisely what the 'portioun usit and wont' had been, whether in money or victual, and if the latter what was the valuation of the victual. But Dean John had his facts and figures. His procurator produced evidence before the Court of Session of what the portion should have been - so much in meal, so much in 'beir' or barley, so much in cash - and the Court accepted it. They even allowed old Dean John's 'oath of verity' as to the precise amounts to be taken on commission in consideration of 'the greate aige and waikness of the said Deane Johne'. It appears that the old man had retired to Dumfries, for it was there that his oath was ordered to be taken. A month later, the certificate of his oath being produced before the Lords, they awarded him his whole claim, amounting to £722 6s. 8d., besides ordering Cassillis to pay him £10 of expenses. This very substantial sum must have assured the comfort of Dean John's last days. [17]

His colleague Dean Gilbert Kennedy was still alive as late as 1607, when we find record of his borrowing some money from a man in Maybole. Since his obligation describes him as 'Deane Gilbert Kennedy in Corsraguell' it is evident that he was still residing in the abbey. [18] The buildings were still sound enough for King James to have toyed in 1602 with the notion of restoring them as an official residence for his eldest son, Henry, Prince and Steward of Scotland, who was also Earl of Carrick, 'quhen he salhappin to resorte in thai pairtes'.[19] But this project was never pursued.

Since Dean Gilbert Kennedy had been a monk of Crossraguel under Abbot Quintin Kennedy before 1560, in 1607 he can hardly have been less than 70 years old, a very great age for those days. Twenty years before, in 1587, he had been censured by the General Assembly for 'profaning the Sacraments' by baptizing children 'in privit houses and fields';[20] for Parliament had in 1567 forbidden any but those 'admittit and havand power to that effect' - in other words, ministers of the Reformed Church - to administer baptism. But this incident, and his obligation of 1607, are almost the only events of his later life that we know.

He was not quite the last Ayrshire survivor of a religious order, for one of the Black Friars of Ayr, David Alison by name, was still living as late as 1617.[21] But in his own neighbourhood he must have been long remembered as a unique veteran of the old times. The incident of 1587 suggests that a younger generation, bringing their children to Dean Gilbert for baptism, regarded him with respect and affection; and I fancy that he is anonymously commemorated in the names 'the Dean's mill' and 'the Dean's meadow' which survived on the maps of the farms around the abbey ruins for well over two centuries after his death.

If he was given to reminiscence in his old age, Dean Gilbert must have had a great fund of anecdote to draw upon. The older brethren at the time of his novitiate would have recalled for him the arrival of the dreadful news of Pinkie, from which so many friends and neighbours had not returned, and the first singing of dirges and requiem masses for them. They must have carefully described to him, too, the stately ritual, five months after the battle, with which Quintin Kennedy, the last abbot of Crossraguel, had been installed in office: an occasion that must have grown more and more splendid in retrospect as the drab years rolled over the decaying abbey in which there were no longer offices said nor anthems sung. They would have gone over, stage by stage, the reading of the mandate from the Bishop of Dunkeld, father abbot of the order of Cluny in Scotland, the presentation to the new abbot by the sub-prior of the abbey's relics and the keys of the whole convent, the high mass, the solemn procession conducting the abbot to his seat in the choir and thereafter to his carved central chair in the beautiful little square chapter-house; not forgetting the three notaries framing a legal record of the whole proceeding, and the congregation crowding church and cloister to watch it all, prominent among them the abbot's elder brother the Earl of Cassillis and a group of local lairds.[22]

Dean Gilbert would clearly remember Abbot Quintin Kennedy, the graduate of St. Andrews and Paris, aristocrat, scholar, and doughty champion of the old Church. He upheld the Scriptural warrant of the mass by preaching, pamphlet, and disputation, the latter maintained for three days in September 1562 in Maybole face to face with John Knox himself, and managed to preserve his abbey almost undamaged although the zealous Reformers from the north, formally rather than physically, 'cast down' a part of its church. It must have been largely through his influence that the Reformation made at first only slow headway in Carrick. In the first General Assembly in December 1560 it was a matter of complaint that the mass was still being celebrated in Crossraguel and in its dependent parish kirks of Maybole, Girvan, Kirkoswald, and Dailly, as well as in the houses of Lord Cassillis and the laird of Kirkmichael.[23] The abbey's wide lands, which the brethren had farmed so well and made so covetable a prize, Abbot Quintin prudently let to his powerful nephew the Earl of Cassillis, and he lived on in his tall, comfortable house in the south-east corner of the precinct, and died there in 1564. Dean Gilbert could himself remember, in contrast to the ceremonies and the rejoicings with which Abbot Quintin had been welcomed, the chilly reception of Master Allan Stewart, the commendator to whom Queen Mary granted the abbey in 1565 as an obligement to his kinsman James Stewart of Cardonald, the Captain of her archer guard.[24] It had been a farcically unimpressive occasion, and surely an annoying disappointment for the pushing young courtier, of dubious descent from an illegitimate offshoot of the house of Lennox[25], who had secured the post of 'furriour' or quartermaster of the newly raised archer guard[26] and from that stepping-stone at Court had at one stride grasped one of the richest monastic estates of the south-west. One December morning of 1565 he rode up to the abbey gate attended by a party of friends and servants and a notary public, bringing with him the royal letters under the Queen's Privy Seal and the letters of provision from the Archbishop of St. Andrews entitling him to take possession of the abbey and its lands. He wished no doubt to be received with all the deference and ceremony due to 'the Lord Commendator', as he styled himself. But if he expected to find the sub-prior and brethren waiting in a submissive group at the gate, a respectful welcome, a formal induction, the abbot's house prepared for his lodging, and a cup of mulled wine by a blazing fire after his cold morning ride, he found nothing of the kind. In fact he was not welcomed at all. Five years before the community had numbered nine brethren, apart from the lay-brothers. This winter morning the abbey buildings appeared to be deserted.

Exploring the abbey, however, the Commendator discovered at last one monk, Dean Michael Dewar, and obliged him to go through the ceremonies which should properly have been conducted by the sub-prior-showing him the entrance to the church, placing him in the abbot's stall, and reading the letters of induction. Dean Michael led him into the chapter-house, the refectory, and finally the abbot's house, and the Commendator, having thus inspected his new possession, left some of his servants in charge of it and departed. The notary's official record of the proceedings implies that they were the coldest and most unenthusiastic formalities.[27] It is clear that Dean Gilbert and all the other brethren had deliberately absented themselves; and the solitary presence of Dean Michael Dewar, who had been in the abbey since 1547 at least and was probably the oldest of the community, implies something else. It was the rule of the Cluniac order that a novice seeking admission to it was received with a show of great reluctance. After being kept a long time waiting at the gate, he was at last admitted not as a welcome guest but as a stranger, and put under the tutelage of the oldest monks in the monastery to be instructed in the severest of their rules. Allan Stewart's chilling reception at Crossraguel suggested, and in all probability was ironically planned to suggest, that the monks regarded him not as their superior but as a suppliant novice. His abbacy did him little good, Dean Gilbert might have reflected. For one thing, the Queen granted Master George Buchanan, the scholar, poet and historian, a pension of £500 a year out of the abbey's resources. For another, only a few months after Stewart had received his grant she allowed the Earl of Cassillis to have a renewal, for 19 years, of the lease of the abbey lands which he had had from his late uncle Abbot Quintin, including the 'abbey place, housis, yardis and pertinentis', thus virtually annulling or superseding the grant to the Commendator. Cassillis was little disposed to respect the Commendator's rights and to see the abbey and its lands which two Kennedy abbots had ruled feed the fortunes of an upstart - even if the latter had married a sister of the Earl of Eglinton.[28] In August 1566 he began to make free with the abbey buildings, sending his chamberlain with several men to despoil 'the houss under the hey houss of the said place of Corsragwell and wallis thairof' of its rafters and flooring - 'diverss geistis and treis of syndrie peices'.[29] He pressed the Commendator to give him a feu charter of the abbey lands. But Stewart was assiduously granting feus and tacks of the lands to various neighbours, his only interest in them being to turn them into cash for the benefit of himself and his kinsman Cardonald. In 1570 Cassillis kidnapped him, carried him off to Dunure, and by torturing him before a great fire enforced his signature to the desired charter. Even in those lawless days this behaviour provoked scandal, and Cassillis spent some time in ward in Dumbarton castle. But he got his way. The Commendator parted with what was left of the lands in return for considerable sums of money, and by the time of his death in 1587 there was little left of the former Crossraguel possessions beyond the abbey buildings.

Even the 'yards' around the abbey which the surviving monks had continued to possess were alienated a few years later. In 1602 King James, who quite often did generous actions, especially when they cost him nothing, made a grant to a certain John Gray, the son of his former nurse Helen Little, of all the abbey gardens. The grant included 'the pasture within all the limits and bounds of the foresaid monastery's precincts, closes, and walls' - an indication of how thickly the grass was by now growing in the cloister and courtyards, and of how much of the outer boundary wall had fallen or been pulled down.[30]

Gray took sasine in one of the gardens ('for they all lie contiguously') on a September afternoon, and 'Dean Gilbert Kennedy, monk in Corsraguell', was one of the witnesses present. Perhaps he did not mind the loss of his garden much. He was too old to dig and weed it now.

Dean Gilbert would remember the year 1587 well. That was the year the Commendator died, a poor man for all his scheming, a mere tenant of the laird of Bargany, at his farm of Glendrissaig near Girvan.[31]

The King conferred the vacant commendatorship, for what it was worth, on John Vaus younger of Barnbarroch. That was the year, too, of Dean Gilbert's own particular trouble when he was censured by the General Assembly. And it was the year of the Queen's execution in England, after which Lord Maxwell raised the standard of revolt in Dumfriesshire, hoping for support from the King of Spain, was besieged by King James's forces in Lochmaben castle, fled by sea to Ailsa Craig, and crossing to the Carrick coast came for refuge to Crossraguel. Denied admittance there he went to an inn in Maybole where he was flushed by his pursuers and finally captured in a wood near by.

But that was twenty years ago. And now they were all dead, these troublers of the peace of Crossraguel, except the present Earl of Cassillis, whom Dean John Bryce had worsted in the Court of Session, and the King who had gone off to enjoy his new English kingdom: all gone to their account - the blustering and blasphemous Knox, and the cruel Cassillis, and the grasping but luckless Commendator, and the Queen who had given him the abbey, and Cardonald, and Master George Buchanan. And Bargany, who had rescued the Commendator out of Dunure, was dead too, and his handsome young son whom the present Cassillis had slain on a dark, wintry day as he rode home from Ayr, after years of feud and broil all over Carrick.

But old Dean Gilbert had outlived them all, and still had his familiar chamber and his 'portioun usit and wont', and his friends, and his leisurely walks out to Maybole, and his memories of good Abbot Quintin; even though the abbey's roofs were falling in, and its fish-ponds silting up, and John Gray's sheep were wandering among its buildings, and its mill and fields and meadows and woods and coal-heughs had passed to strangers.

1. *Statistical Account of Scotland*, x, p. 494, note.

2 *Crossraguel Charters*, ii, p. 89; cp. *New Statistical Account of Scotland*, v (Ayrshire), p. 782.

3 *Crossraguel Charters*, ii, p. 112.

4 Mr. F. C. Hunter Blair (1859-1940).

5 See Gordon Donaldson, 'The Parish Clergy and the Reformation " in *The Innes Review*, x, pp.13-14.

6 *Macfarlane's Geographical Collections* (Scottish History Society), ii, p.257.

7 *History of the Reformation in Scotland*, ed. Dickinson, i, p. 364.

8 Protocol Book of Henry Prestoun, f. 6

9 *Crossraguel Charters*, i, pp. 40, 124.

10 *Ibid.*, i, p. xlvii.

11 *Booke of the Universall Kirk*, i, p. 5.

12 *Crossraguel Charters*, ii, p. 64.

13 Register of Deeds, lxviii, ff. 2-3.

14 *Ibid.*, lix, f. 394.

15 *Historie of the Kennedyis*, p. 19.

16 Register of Deeds, lxxiv, f. 363.

17 Acts and Decreets, ccii, ff. 6-7, 297-8.

18 Register of Deeds, cxlix, ff. 285-6.

19 *Crossraguel Charters*, ii, p. 69.

20 *Ibid.*, p. 58.

21 *The Royal Burgh of Ayr*, ed. Dunlop, p. 99.

22 *Protocol Book of Henry Prestoun*, f. 6.

23 *Booke of the Universall Kirk*, i, p. 5.

24 *R.S.S.*, v, 2187; D. Hay Fleming, *Mary, Queen of Scots*, p. 271.

25 He was probably an illegitimate son of Cardonald who was illegitimately descended from the 1st Earl of Lennox (*Scots Peerage*, v, p. 350), but his parentage is never more precisely stated than 'born of a noble family' (*Crossraguel Charters*, i, p. 144).

26 *R.S.S.*, v, 1368.

27 *Crossraguel Charters*, i, pp. 146-9.

28 A sister of Lady Bargany (*Historie of the Kennedyis*, pp. 9-10), who was Lady Agnes Montgomerie. Her sister Lady Jean is stated to have been contracted in 1560 to a son of James Stewart of Cardonald, named (presumably in error) Matthew Stewart: no son of Cardonald's of that name is otherwise recorded. (*Memorials of the Montgomeries*, ii, p. 160.) Allan Stewart was certainly married for he left three' lauchfull dochteris' (Edinburgh Testaments, xix, f. 186).

29 Acts and Decreets, xl, f. 129.

30 *R.M.S.*, vi, 1328; Secretary's Register of Sasines, Ayr, ii, ff. 29-30.

31 Edinburgh Testaments, xix, f. 186.

5

Master Robert Cathcart of Pinmore and the Carrick Feud

One of the unrecognized masterpieces of Scottish vernacular literature is the *Historie of the Kennedyis*. The probable reason why it is so little known is that the only publication of it, edited by the learned and industrious Robert Pitcairn, was over 130 years ago, in a small impression which was never reprinted and has now become extremely rare. Another possible explanation is that the only manuscript of it, which is in the National Library of Scotland, breaks off in mid-paragraph at one of the most exciting moments in the story, so that as a work of literature the *Historie* is incomplete.

It is none the less an historical memoir of the highest value. The anonymous author, obviously himself a Carrick man and acquainted with many of the principal figures in his story, narrates the rise of the Kennedys in Ayrshire, the elevation of the Kennedys of Dunure to be first Lords Kennedy and later Earls of Cassillis, and then, in careful and vivid detail, the saga of their great feud with their kinsmen the Kennedys of Bargany. The surviving text fortunately includes the climax of the struggle - the battle at Brockloch, near Maybole, on 11 December 1601, in which the young laird of Bargany, Gilbert Kennedy, was mortally wounded; and its sequels of revenge, the murder of Sir Thomas Kennedy of Culzean and the burning of the house of Auchinsoull. There is no fuller account of any of the great family vendettas which bedevilled the Scotland of the late sixteenth century.

The *Historie* has naturally been used as a source-book by James Paterson the historian of Ayrshire and by everyone since his time who has written on the county's early history. It has also been a quarry for novelists, notably S. R. Crockett for *The Grey Man*. These borrowings are not surprising, for the unknown author had a fascinating style. He writes in Scots, the tongue which was in his day losing ground in literature but was still generally used in legal documents and in all private correspondence. He has a racy vocabulary and a pithy turn of phrase contrasting strongly with the rambling periods of some of his contemporaries. Generally his style is colloquial, not quite that of a letter but rather of a man talking; yet on occasions he rises to a studied eloquence, notably in his account of the fight at Brockloch, which is a really magnificent battlepiece, full of sharply observed details and vivid touches of characterization.

As history particularly, the work is illuminating to those who know the historical map of Carrick. The district has been very little changed by modern industrial or housing developments, and even today the countryside is full of visible memorials of the stories of the Kennedy feud. The old castles of Bargany and Blairquhan, Culzean and Auchindrane, have vanished, it is true, having all been rebuilt. Dunure and Craigneill, Baltersan and Thomastoun are only shells, and Ardstinchar a mere fragment, though each of them retains some ghostly grandeur of its past. But the Earl of Cassillis's great houses in Maybole and at Cassillis itself still stand inhabited and scarcely altered, as does the Cathcarts' tower of Killochan; and Ardmillan, as already mentioned, also survives. The buildings of Crossraguel Abbey are, though ruined and mostly roofless, more complete than those of any other monastic foundation in Scotland except Inchcolm. Beside the old moorland road from Maybole to Dailly, now used only by shepherds and gamekeepers, you can still see, somewhat subsided into the heather, the cairn marking the spot where Kennedy of Girvanmains ambushed and slew McAlexander of Drummochreen. You may still stand on the high-arched bridge of Doon over which young Bargany rode to his death three hundred and sixty years ago. And in the kirkyard of Ballantrae, below the steep craig on which his castle of Ardstinchar stood, is the aisle, somewhat weathered but today well preserved, containing the 'glorious tomb' which Bargany's widow made for him and in which her body was so soon afterwards laid beside his in September 1605.

Every page of the *Historie* shows that its author knew the topography of Carrick intimately. He is moreover an obvious partisan of the Bargany family. His affection for them appears several times. On the death of the old laird of Bargany, in the key year of 1597 when the final and fatal stage of the great feud begins, he gives a long and dignified eulogy of 'the nobillest man that ever was in that cuntry in his tyme'. On the death of the old Lady Bargany, too, he commemorates her as 'ane nobill womane ... maist nobill in all hir effairis'. Young Bargany, the only person whose physical appearance he describes in detail, is obviously the hero of his whole story; and his widow, as I shall explain later, is treated with particular sympathy. On the other hand the author makes no secret of his loathing for the fifth Earl of Cassillis who brought about young Bargany's death, nor of his contempt for Bargany's pusillanimous kinsmen Bennan and Ardmillan. The whole story is seen through the eyes of a devoted, loyal, and even prejudiced Bargany supporter.

Who was he? His Bargany sympathies are the essential point to consider in speculating about his identity. Yet they have been underestimated in the only two theories of authorship which have yet been suggested. Pitcairn, editing the *Historie* for publication in 1830, gave reasons why he was 'at one time convinced' that the author was that sinuous politician John Mure of Auchindrane, Bargany's brother-in-law, because of his prominence in the narrative and the frequent reproduction of his exact words in conversation. Pitcairn does not say why he changed his opinion; and there is another explanation, as I shall show, for Auchindrane's prominence in the story. Paterson, the county historian, disagreed, on the grounds that Auchindrane could not have been a well enough educated man to have written the *Historie*, and put forward a theory that the author was Auchindrane's kinsman Master Robert Mure, the schoolmaster of Ayr.[1] There is no evidence of any kind to support this fancy. But Paterson was on the right track. The author of the *Historie* was undoubtedly an educated man; and this narrows the field of inquiry to a very encouraging degree.

But there is no help to be got from the manuscript itself. Examination of it makes quite clear that it is not the author's original but a contemporary copy by some other hand. It is rather strange that Pitcairn should have either failed to notice this or not thought it worth mentioning. The copyist is plainly not a Carrick man himself; for he makes several mistakes in copying place-names,[2] leaves a few blank spaces where he has altogether failed to read others, and dates the Earl of Cassillis's return from France, which was in 1597, as in 1565 (which would be about three years before he was born). In many places he has evidently been unable to read the manuscript before him and has omitted words and even whole phrases, leaving blanks never filled in. His own handwriting is very bad and not easy to read. Pitcairn's transcript is far from perfect and cannot have been collated, for he miscopies some words, omits some others, often vital to the sense, and in one place leaves out a whole line. In fact a new edition of the *Historie of the Kennedyis* is much to be desired. The history of the copy-manuscript is itself something of a puzzle. There is no indication why the writing should break off where it does -whether the original really stopped at that point or the copyist simply became tired of it. The writing, which is continuous and unparagraphed throughout, ends a little way down the verso of a page, and somewhat lower down there begins, in a different handwriting, an account of the state and government of Spain. Finally, to add to the mysteries, the two outer leaves enclosing the manuscript, on the back of one of which the last part of the description of Spain is written, are part of an English legal document in an English hand.

We come back therefore to the internal evidence of the manuscript. Its contents, including those parts which, as they do not concern the Kennedys, Pitcairn did not print, make it clear that the author was, to the best of his ability, a serious historian. His writing of the *Historie* was a deflection from the ambitious task on which he originally set out, and is really a very long parenthesis in it. The manuscript begins with the title 'The Descriptioun of Scotland with ane Cronickell off the Kingis thair Lyff and Descent', and opens with about thirty closely written pages of annals, beginning with the reign of the mythical King Gatheilus, husband of the Princess Scota, the supposed eponymous ancestress of the Scots. Then follow eight pages of more detailed history and another sixteen of annals of the author's own time brought down to 1611, which year is thus a *terminus a quo* by which to date the whole composition. The last episode described is the reorganization of the Privy Council after the Earl of Dunbar's death, which was on 20 January 1611.

We then get thirty-five pages of miscellaneous matter. There is a list of the sheriffdoms of Scotland, short lives of the Regents, a topographical description of Scotland similar to Buchanan's but not copied from him, and lastly an account of the origins of the principal Scottish families or 'names', the material for which the author states to have been taken from 'my copy quhilk I drew out of the blak buik of

Skoun'. It was this section of the work which, so to speak, led the author astray. When he arrives at the name of Kennedy - to which he has already given significant attention in his brief account of the country of Carrick - he embarks on his long diversion with this excuse: 'Seeing that thair is sum noittis for memory heirefter to follow off the name of Kennedy I thocht gude to conteyne heir thair beginning and how thay roiss to be gritt and sa furthe to this hour.'

Now the author has obviously read Buchanan and other historical writers. He mentions a 'Chronicle', otherwise unidentified. He has had access to the lost Black Book of Scone and copied out some of it. He knows what he calls 'Wallace buik'. A chance allusion among the family histories shows that he has read Chaucer. Further, the details he gives of the deaths of both young Bargany and his wife suggest that he has some pretensions to a knowledge of medicine.

It can be said without hesitation that there were extremely few men in Carrick in the early seventeenth century - indeed a mere handful - likely to be so well read; and in considering who was this anonymous author we can at once leave several of them out of consideration: the schoolmaster of Maybole, the various notaries, and the seven parish ministers, or rather the three - Mr. David Barclay at Dailly and later at Maybole, Mr. John Maccorn first at Maybole and later at Straiton, and Mr. John Cunynghame at Girvan - who were in their charges throughout the events described. For it is abundantly clear that the author was, if not a laird himself, a member of one of the principal landed families in Carrick, acquainted with the chief characters in his story and moving as an equal among them; and his view of his subject is certainly not that of a minister, nor of a notary.

I assume as a probability amounting to a certainty that our well-read author had studied at a university. By no means every man who matriculated in those days went on to take a degree. A recorded list of heritors and 'weill landit men' in the parish of Kirkoswald in 1607, which includes several prominent local lairds,[3] comprises twenty names not one of which has the prefix 'Mr.' indicating that its bearer was a Master of Arts, which in legal documents is never omitted. A careful listing of Carrick lairds and their kinsmen living between 1595 and 1610 who were Masters of Arts collects only six names. But among those six there appears one man who could have been, and I venture to think was, the author of the *Historie of the Kennedyis*. The other five, at any rate, can be dismissed without hesitation.

I eliminate first Master Lambert Kennedy of Kirkmichael, who made singularly little mark on his times. He is nowhere mentioned in the records of Parliament or of the Privy Council, and though he occasionally figures in records and other documents as a witness he practically never appears as cautioner, executor, tutor, or arbitrator. He certainly took no part in public life in Carrick, and I deduce that he was either an invalid or a recluse.

Master Alexander Boyd, brother of the laird of Penkill, was a man of great learning, a traveller, and a poet - remembered today for one incomparable sonnet, 'Fra bank to bank, fra wood to wood I rin'. But he died in 1601, before half the events of the feud recorded in the *Historie* had taken place. Master John Fergusson of Kilkerran, on the other hand, did not graduate till 1610 and was only a boy during most of our period. Master John Chalmer of Sandifurd, a kinsman of the Boyds of Trochraig and Penkill, was undoubtedly a Cassillis adherent; and so was Master Christopher Cockburn, who was in the Earl of Cassillis's service and was among his party in the crucial battle in 1601.[4]

If the author is among these six, therefore, there is only one possible candidate: Master Robert Cathcart of Nether Pinmore, second son of John Cathcart of Carleton. Not much can be discovered about him. He appears a few times in the Register of the Privy Council, as a witness to various documents recorded in the Books of Council and Session, and in two or three testaments. But the contexts in which his name appears nearly all connect him with some of the leading figures in the *Historie of the Kennedyis*; and I believe him to have been its author.

Let us again summarize what we have hitherto deduced about this author's position, personality, and attitude. He was a gentleman, and well educated. He belonged to Carrick, and was especially familiar with the country around and between its two rivers, the Water of Girvan and the Water of Stinchar. He does not seem to have been himself a Kennedy; for though he often refers to the cadets of the family, calling them 'the

Freindis' - that is, the kinsmen - he never says 'we'. Yet he was certainly intimate with the family of Kennedy of Bargany and knew their history well; for he gives what may be called the Bargany version of the roasting of Allan Stewart, commendator of Crossraguel, in the castle of Dunure and of his rescue thence by Bargany's men; he has detailed knowledge of old Bargany's dealings with the fourth Earl of Cassillis and with the lairds of Culzean and Auchindrane; he has witnessed the lordly housekeeping in the castle of Bargany in the old laird's time; and, as already mentioned, he loves and idealizes the young laird Gilbert who came so early to a tragic end.

Further, the author plainly has, for Gilbert's sake perhaps, a particular interest in his wife Jonet Stewart. Their marriage had been imposed on the family in 1597 by King James's order, which to a great baron like old Bargany, who might expect to choose his own alliances, was humiliating. It was, says the author, 'ane gritt wrak to his hous' - but he adds ' -uther nor he gatt ane gude womane'. He pays close attention to young Lady Bargany's fortunes after her husband's murder. He describes her 'great anger' at the Earl of Cassillis's evading of all penalty for Bargany's death; her efforts to organize revenge for it; her fatal illness, the exact date and place of her death, which are recorded nowhere else, and her funeral. On all these points, wherever he can be checked, he is strikingly accurate, as indeed he is on a large number of others in the *Historie* once it reaches the period under his observation, a circumstance which makes one the more inclined to trust him where he is the sole witness.

Next, the author is, as Pitcairn noted, very intimate with the laird of Auchindrane, John Mure, and remarkably conversant with his movements and actions, and even his exact words. He is equally well informed, though Pitcairn did not observe it, about the laird of Carleton, John Cathcart, and his eldest son (Master Robert Cathcart's father and brother). The brother - John Cathcart younger of Carleton - was present at a vital conference of the Bargany faction in Ardstinchar castle, and also in the battle at Brockloch. He, just as much as Auchindrane, could have been the author's informant regarding both occasions, which are described in great detail.

Finally, though the author tells us nothing directly about himself, we can infer his principles in Church matters; for he calls Quintin Kennedy, the last abbot of Crossraguel, 'ane gude man, and ane that feiritt God efter the maner of his religione', and of old Bargany, who had been an active Reformer, he says that he 'was fra the beginning on the rycht syd of religioun'.

It does not seem that the *Historie* was meant for a wide audience. As I have already mentioned, its style is not literary but informal. It makes virtually no reference to national affairs - not even to King James's succession to the English Crown and his departure from Scotland. It is local history, indeed clan history, written entirely for readers who already know the scene, the outline, and the chief characters. My guess is that it was intended for the family charter-chest at Killochan, and that, but for the destruction of those archives about fifty years ago, the original might have been found there. But at any rate the author's attitude to his theme and his audience emphasize the certainty that he was a Carrick man and closely associated with the house of Bargany.

The career of Master Robert Cathcart fits strikingly well into this framework. He was born in all probability at Killochan, the home of his father John Cathcart of Carleton, whose wife was Helen Wallace. Killochan stands today just as it stood in Robert's youth (his parents rebuilt or enlarged it in 1586), unaltered but for the addition of an eighteenth-century wing, occupied, and admirably preserved. It lies near the Water of Girvan, about three miles from its mouth, little over a mile from the site of the old castle of Bargany and about an hour's ride from Maybole. Robert's parents were married in about 1563[5] and he was probably born in 1565, certainly not more than a year or so later. He was thus about 32 in the momentous year of 1597 when old Bargany died and the young Earl of Cassillis came home from France, and about 36 when young Gilbert Kennedy of Bargany met his end.

It must have been at Glasgow that he took his Master of Arts degree. The university's records are deficient for this period so that we do not know the date but may presume it to have been about 1582, the year in which Edinburgh University was founded. He married soon afterwards, at the age of about twenty.

Master Robert's wife was Agnes Kennedy, a widow with a young family, and she was perhaps a little older than himself, though not certainly: girls married very young in those days. Her first husband, who had died in February 1581, was John Eccles of Kildonan, and he left her with one daughter of her own, Agnes, and the guardianship of his other daughters by an earlier marriage and one bastard daughter. The Eccles and Cathcart families must have been on friendly terms, for the laird of Kildonan's will includes the sentence, 'Item he levis the young laird of Cairltoun his hagbut and tua pistolattis'.[6] This acquaintanceship easily accounts for Master Robert's having married Kildonan's widow Agnes Kennedy and settled down with her at Kildonan in the Stinchar valley, where we next hear of him in 1593. Three days before Christmas in that year Agnes died.

Master Robert's marriage had lasted only some eight years (presuming that he had married at about twenty). The terms of Agnes Kennedy's will suggest that it had been a happy one. She appointed her husband her sole executor, left him to divide her personal property among their children, and committed to him the tutorship of his step-daughter Agnes Eccles, 'faitherlie to governe hir as his awin'.[7] The testament mentions 'barnes' of hers and Robert's, but names only the eldest son John.

Within the next three years Master Robert bought the small estate of Nether Pinmore a little further up the Stinchar, and he is always described hereafter as either 'of Nether Pinmore' or 'of Pinmore'. He did not marry again. It may have been about this time that he formed a friendship with a young neighbour of the Cathcarts, Master Robert Boyd of Trochrig, who went to France in 1597 and there won celebrity as a philosopher and theologian, returning to Scotland in 1614 to become a famous Principal of Glasgow University; for on Master Robert's death Boyd mourned him as an old friend and as 'a man of great piety and experience in the way and life of God'.[8]

During the four crucial years of the Kennedy feud, from 1597 to 1601, Master Robert Cathcart is scarcely on record at all. His name is not mentioned in the *Historie* during that or any other period. But his father and elder brother appear in it several times, and, as I have already remarked, would have been first-hand sources for many of the principal events in the feud. Indeed the house of Killochan is admirably placed to have been a centre for the hearing and reporting of news of all Kennedy doings: close to Bargany, not far from Maybole to the north-east or the bridge of Girvan to the south-west, and forming one link in that chain of towers and manor-houses, nearly all belonging to Kennedys, which stretched all down the Girvan Water for more than a dozen miles.

In the battle of 11 December 1601 when Bargany got his mortal wound, Master Robert's elder brother John commanded the main body of his followers, wearing, perhaps, the pistols he had inherited from the laird of Kildonan. It is in the weeks immediately following that tragedy that Master Robert appears on record again, and it is these appearances that seem to me significant.

'The Lady Barganie,' says the writer of the *Historie*, 'raid to Edinburgh and maid hir complent to the King and Queine, bot wes littill the better ... for scho wes compellit to by the ward of hir sone, and to gif threttene thousand markis for the same.' That she did go to Edinburgh and that she did have. to buy the wardship of her own son is perfectly true. The payment of the composition is recorded in the unprinted accounts of the Lord Treasurer, and the grant of the ward in the unprinted Register of the Privy Seal, dated 14 January 1602, just five months after Bargany's death. But the sum which the Lord Treasurer received, or at any rate the sum for which he accounted, was not 13,000 merks but 10,000.[9]

Yet Lady Bargany's total expenses on this unrewarding journey to Edinburgh may very well have included another 3,000 merks. There would be her travelling and lodging expenses, some legal fees to pay, and not improbably some *douceurs* necessary to enable her to reach Royalty's unsympathetic ear - even though she had been one of Queen Anne's maids of honour less than five years before. What is certain is that while she was in Edinburgh, six days after the grant of her wardship, she had to borrow the large sum of £816, equal to over 1,200 merks.[10] And there was one man well placed to know her financial difficulties at this very time - Master Robert Cathcart; for he was one of the witnesses to the bond for £816 which Lady Bargany signed on 20 January 1602. He was by no means the only person available for this purpose, for Fergus Kennedy of Knockdaw, who had been close behind Bargany when he was wounded, Knockdaw's brother, and another Kennedy laird, Hew of Clauchantoun, were all in Edinburgh at this time.[11] It would seem that Lady Bargany regarded Master Robert Cathcart as a closer friend than any of these, and that he, a friend and neighbour of the Bargany family but one who had not himself been active in the feud and so was not being pursued by the vengeance of the Earl of Cassillis or the Privy Council, had ridden to Edinburgh with Bargany's widow to stand by her in her trouble.

The authorities took note of his sympathies a few months later. In the interval, on 12 May 1602, Lord Cassillis's uncle, Sir Thomas Kennedy of Culzean, had been murdered by Bargany's young brother, Thomas Kennedy of Drummurchie, and his friend Walter Mure of Cloncaird, in revenge for Bargany's death. The murderers were outlawed, and all the prominent men of the Bargany faction were required by the Privy Council to find caution not to reset them - that is, not to give them countenance or shelter. They almost all complied, for 'thair wes ane gritt feir in all mennis hairttis'. One of those from whom this guarantee was demanded was 'Mr. Robert Cathcart of Penmoir'. He and Fergus Kennedy of Knockdaw were mutual cautioners for each other, both their bonds being signed at Killochan on 22 September.[12]

That was not the only indication in this year of 1602 of where Master Robert's sympathies lay. On 28 January, only seven weeks after the battle and while Lord Cassillis was in Edinburgh justifying himself before the Privy Council,[13] Master Robert had returned to Ayrshire and was at the house of Auchindrane, in company with Cloncaird (the future assassin of Sir Thomas Kennedy of Culzean) and Auchindrane himself; for he and Cloncaird were two (if the witnesses to a bond which Auchindrane signed on that day.[14] This was another time when Master Robert could have heard first-hand accounts of the battle, for both Cloncaird and Auchindrane had been prominent in it on Bargany's side. Cloncaird had killed Lord Cassillis's master of household, and Auchindrane had received a severe wound from the shot of a hackbut. It is noteworthy that the Historie gives the whole conversation between Bargany and Auchindrane when the latter tried to persuade the young man to turn back on his fatal journey, and describes how Auchindrane got his wound, his danger from it, and the relations in the next few weeks between him, Cloncaird, Drummurchie, and Lady Bargany, who, it says, was 'dealing with' Cloncaird and Drummurchie to concert plans for Culzean's murder. If Master Robert was not himself involved in these plots he was undoubtedly in very close contact with those who were. And the writer of the *Historie* certainly knew Cloncaird and had a liking for him. 'He was bayth stout and kynd,' he says; 'and giff that he had had dayis, wald have beine ane verry fyne man.'

There was another episode about this time of which Master Robert might have been an eyewitness. It also happened while Lord Cassillis was still in Edinburgh. For some time after the fight of 11 December 1601 Auchindrane was laid up, recovering from his wound; but he was evidently up and about again when Sir Thomas Kennedy of Culzean sought his help. Culzean was connected with Auchindrane since they were cousins by marriage and moreover Auchindrane's eldest son had married Culzean's daughter only a little over a year before.[15] Auchindrane himself was married to Bargany's sister. He therefore had a foot in both camps, and Culzean quite reasonably asked him to act as mediator between himself and Drummurchie and Cloncaird, who he had heard were plotting at Lady Bargany's instigation to murder him.

Auchindrane agreed to do his best, procured proposals from both sides for a kind of treaty of future neutrality in the feud, got Drummurchie and Cloncaird to come to his house, and then invited Culzean to dinner to meet them. When Culzean arrived. Auchindrane talked to him in the hall. having persuaded the other two to wait upstairs 'in ane chalmer'. But Culzean changed his mind, and said he could not enter into any agreement without his chief's knowledge and consent. He took his leave, and Auchindrane politely saw him home almost all the way to Culzean.

Now this whole episode is reported in the *Historie* in great detail. with the actual conversation of Auchindrane and his guest, which gives a very strong impression of being more than Auchindrane's own account. in fact the account of an eyewitness. In other words, it looks as if the writer of the *Historie* was himself present. We know that Master Robert Cathcart was on visiting terms with Auchindrane at just this time. We know that on one occasion at just this time he was in Auchindrane's house in company with Cloncaird. He may therefore very well have been the person who witnessed and recorded this abortive attempt to limit the progress of the Carrick vendetta.

The Cassillis party, however, had the upper hand by this time. and Master Robert's father, the laird of Carleton, 'maid moyane', says the *Historie*, 'nocht to be trublitt nor to trubill'. In the spring of 1603 occurred the last attempt of the Bargany faction to avenge their lost chief. Drummurchie and Cloncaird besieged Lord Cassillis's wife and brother with their attendants in the house of Auchinsoull beside the Stinchar and very nearly caught the man who had actually given Bargany his death-wound, but he got away under cover of the smoke from the burning house. This episode, most vividly described in the *Historie*, took place only four miles up the Stinchar from Master Robert's house of Pinmore, so that he could have had ample opportunities of hearing all its details from his neighbours.

We find a record of him next in 1605, and again in close association with the widowed Lady Bargany. Early in July she was in Edinburgh. She was now a dying woman, suffering from what was probably tuberculosis - called in those days a hectic fever, or in the words of the *Historie* 'the eittik'. She was about to set out for London to consult the Queen's physician, Dr. Martin;[16] and before her departure she assigned the management of all her affairs to her brother Josias Stewart of Bonytoun. She was 'very far gevin over to his counsell', says the *Historie*, and there is evidence suggesting that his advice concerning the management of the Bargany estates was un-businesslike.[17] The author of the *Historie* writes of it somewhat critically. Master Robert Cathcart was in a position to know something about it, for he was a witness to the five documents which Lady Bargany signed in Edinburgh on 6 July.[18] The same day she made her testament, bravely describing herself as 'haill in bodie and spreit (praisit be God)' and nominating her brother Josias her sole executor. To this document also Master Robert was a witness.[19] Then she set out for London, accompanied by Josias. The Queen's doctor could do nothing for her; 'quhairfoir', says the *Historie*, 'scho wald have beine att hame'. But she was never to see Ayrshire again. On the homeward road, at Stilton, sixty miles from London, she died on 16 August. Josias brought her body by the Sanquhar road to Ayr, and on 15 September[20] the bodies of her husband and herself were solemnly conveyed to Ballantrae and buried in the tomb Lady Bargany had prepared, beneath their stone-carved recumbent effigies. Three Earls, four Lords, and a thousand gentlemen on horseback formed the procession, which included a banner of revenge borne by Bargany's nephew, the son of Auchindrane, showing Bargany's portrait 'with all his woundis' and the motto which customarily went with such devices, 'Judge and revenge my cause, O Lord!' It was all done 'verry honourabilly', as the *Historie* says, and no doubt very expensively too, helping to contribute to the ruin of the Bargany fortunes which followed in a few years.

These matters are described with a detail which, admittedly, many people in Carrick would have known; but the close and compassionate attention paid to the circumstances of young Lady Bargany's death suggests again that the writer was a near friend and probably companion of hers.

Little more is known of Master Robert Cathcart. He died in 1616, for it was in October of that year that his friend the Principal of Glasgow University recorded hearing the news. I was once inclined to doubt this as a false rumour, for five years later there is recorded an allusion to the marriage contract of 'Robert Cathcart of Neddir Pinmoir' and Auchindrane's daughter Elizabeth Mure,[21] and I had assumed that this indicated a late second marriage of Master Robert to a child of his old associate (who, with his eldest son, had been executed for murder in 1611). But as this Robert Cathcart is not designated 'Master' either in this reference or in his appearance as a witness in 1617,[22] I think he must have been one of Master Robert's sons. We know from Agnes Kennedy's testament that he had other children besides John the eldest. Anyhow, this marriage supplies one more fragment of evidence connecting Master Robert's family with that of Auchindrane.

Shadowy though his personality must remain - Robert Boyd's tribute to his piety is the only direct evidence of his character - it is, I think, striking that almost every surviving record of his life associates him with the families of Bargany and Auchindrane. That he did write the *Historie of the Kennedyis* cannot be proved; but it is certain that he could have done so, and that there was no one in Carrick at the time better qualified for the task.

1 James Paterson, *History of the County of Ayr*, i, p. 105.

2 I deduce that what the copyist really had before him, to take a few instances, was Knokdaw for 'Kirkdall', Corsraguell for 'Caragall', Kilhenzie for 'Schalzie' in one place and 'Keilmeny' in another, Grimet for 'Grimak', and Cairltoun for 'Camiltoune'. He fares

no better with Galloway place-names, reading 'Feochtt' for Freuch, 'Barnebarony' for Barnebaroch, 'Gairsland' for Gairthland, and 'Kirkcalffy' for Craigcaffy.

3 Register of Deeds, ccx, ff. 158-60.

4 *Privy Council Register*, vi, pp. 652, 760; *ibid.*, pp. 349, 694.

5 They were already married by 24 September of that year (*R.M.S.*, iv, 1485).

6 Edinburgh Testaments, xiv, ff. 210-11.

7 Edinburgh Testaments, xxvii, ff. 63-4.

8 *Bannatyne Miscellany*, i, p. 288.

9 Treasurer's Accounts, 1601-4, f. 18v; Register of the Privy Seal, vol. lxxii, *sub* 14 January 1602.

10 Register of Deeds, lxxxvi, ff. 103-4.

11 Register of Deeds, cxxxii, ff. 160-1.

12 *P.C.R.*, vi, p. 754.

13 *Ibid.*, pp. 347-50.

14 Register of Deeds, xcii, ff. 291-2.

15 Register of Deeds, xxxiv, ff. 216-18.

16 On whom see *Calendar of State Papers (Domestic)*, 1603-10, pp. 205, 233.

17 Register of Deeds, cvii, ff. 39-41, 129-30, etc.

18 Register of Deeds, cx, ff. 134-8.

19 Glasgow Testaments, xvii, ff. 114-16.

20 The year 1605, left blank in the MS and Pitcairn's text, is confirmed by *Ayr Burgh Accounts* (Scottish History Society), p. 228.

21 Ayr Sasines, ii, ff. 216-17.

22 Kennedy of Bennan MSS (H.M. General Register House), 42.

6

The Fortunes of William Niven

As one of Robert Burns's boyhood friends in his Kirkoswald days, William Niven has a definite if modest place in the poet's biography. To him were written, in 1780-1, the three earliest of Burns's letters known to survive. Another, of 1786, shows that Burns's affection for him lasted into manhood. 'Mr. William Niven, merchant, Maybole' was among the subscribers to the first Edinburgh edition of Burns's poems. It is said that 'subsequently they fell out', and that in later life Niven claimed that it was to himself that Burns's *Epistle to a Young Friend* had originally been addressed - despite the facts that the 'young friend' is specifically named as 'Andrew' and that Burns and Niven were almost exactly of the same age.[1]

Possibly these traditions are groundless. Hardly any of Burns's biographers have traced Niven's successful and to some extent distinguished career beyond his early association with the poet. A generation ago a minister of Kirkoswald, Mr. James Muir, who gathered much information about Burns's Kirkoswald friends into a small book, thus summarized Niven's later life:[2]

'William Niven, it is said, acted as partner with his father, and afterwards as sole partner, in the business at Maybole. On the death of two bachelor brothers in Jamaica, he became possessed of the immense wealth which they had amassed there - £100,000, it is said - and purchased the estate of Kirkbride, near Maybole. Nevertheless, he became hard and parsimonious to a degree. At the mature age of 85, he died 13 December 1844, and lies buried in Maybole churchyard. His portrait, long hanging on the walls of Kirkbride House, is now to be seen in Maybole Town Hall.'

This is not altogether accurate, and a rather fuller account of William Niven can be drawn from information unknown, though mostly quite accessible, to Mr. Muir. As with all biography, the public records are the obvious, though often neglected source. There are also allusions to

Niven in the New Statistical Account of Scotland, and a small bundle of his letters survives among the Hamilton of Pinmore papers in the Register House.

Niven was born in February 1759, the second son of John Niven by his wife Janet Spear. He spent almost his whole life in or near the little town of Maybole. His father was a shopkeeper there and also owned the small neighbouring farm of Kirklandhill. William himself prospered as a merchant and later as a banker. There was some foundation, as I shall show, for the story of the Jamaica inheritance; but like many legacies this one was much smaller in fact than in tradition. It was Niven's industry, with the encouragement and help of a local laird, not the death of rich brothers, that raised him to prosperity and ultimately wealth.

Precisely what help Niven received in early life is uncertain, but it came from Hugh Hamilton of Pinmore, the purchaser of the Pinmore estate in the Stinchar valley. The late owner had been Robert Kennedy of Pinmore, who sold it in 1781;[3] he had been one of the many Ayrshire lairds ruined by the collapse of Douglas, Heron & Company's bank in 1778. James Hunter, who had been their cashier, founded, with the help of his brother and two cousins, the new banking business of Hunters & Company which, much more prudently conducted, flourished for seventy years and was finally merged in the Union Bank of Scotland. Of this bank Hugh Hamilton was one of the directors; and since Niven became its Maybole agent he presumably owed this position to Hamilton's patronage.

At any rate, Niven constantly and gratefully acknowledged the assistance he had had in early life from Mr. Hamilton. In 1810 he wrote of his 'steady, uniform, and essential friendship' which had 'had for its object the improvement of my fortune and respectability in life'. Similarly in 1813 he told Mr. Hamilton, 'You have uniformly been my best and most steady friend. ... You have, Sir, in a great many most essential and important instances paved the way for me, and have enabled me to better my circumstances.' Again, in 1817 he wrote, 'I owe my success in life to your steady and friendly patronage'; and in 1820 he called Hamilton 'my first and best benefactor'. Whatever his faults were, they did not include ingratitude.

He became a partner in Hunters & Company, and in his early thirties began to play a part in the public life of his native town. On 19 March 1792 he and five others were co-opted to the Town Council of Maybole. About the same time, or a year or two later, Niven had prospered enough to build himself a new house on the south side of the High Street. Shortly afterwards he found a mistress for it, a girl named Isabella Christian Goudie, whom he married in Glasgow on 9 September 1798.

Isabella was the daughter of the deceased Robert Goudie, of Kingston, Jamaica. Here, probably, is the origin of the story of the Jamaica fortune. But that rumour exaggerated it is proved by the terms of William's and Isabella's marriage contract. All that he could settle on his bride was a free annuity after his decease of £60 (which he later increased to £120), and the liferent use of his house, furniture, and linen. Isabella herself had a tocher of only £800, and all that ultimately came to her and her husband out of her father's estate was the sum of £471 6s. 10d.[4]

There are other grounds too for doubting the legend of the £100,000. Less than a year after his marriage, Niven bought the farm of Kirkbride and two other small properties in the parish of Kirkmichael, some five miles south of Maybole, which had formed part of the Blairquhan estate and marched with that of Kilkerran. No legacy helped him to make this purchase. In fact he wrote rather doubtfully to Mr. Hamilton about 'making up the money necessary for the purchase which together with your kind assistance I hope I will get accomplished'.

Evidently it was something of an effort for him to buy Kirkbride. He completed the purchase, however, in June 1799 - and in that month he had to borrow £3,000 from Hunters & Company, with 'the two merkland of Kirkbride' itself as security.[5]

It was probably at about the time of his marriage that he had his portrait painted. It shows a cautious face, with a long upper lip and a shrewd, tight mouth, such a countenance as might itself have given rise to the legend of parsimony.

Mrs. Niven lived till 15 February 1841,[6] her husband surviving nearly four years longer. There were no children of the marriage, and late in life Niven could entail his property only on his brother-in-law, John Goudie, who was then living with him, a grand-niece, and a distant cousin, 'Doctor Alexander Niven, late Minister of the Gospel at Dunkeld'.

During the Napoleonic wars Niven's business in Maybole was flourishing and he was playing a leading part in the Town Council, whose meetings he seldom missed. He did various kinds of business for his friend Mr. Hamilton of Pinmore, who in 1810, to Niven's great gratification, recommended him for appointment as one of the Deputy Lieutenants for Ayrshire.

Over the years he acquired considerable landed property, as is shown by the long list of it in his testamentary disposition of 3 September 1841.[7] He added to Kirkbride the farm of Auchalton 'with the lime rock therein' and it presumably was he who worked the limestone quarry still to be seen some way above Auchalton beside the hill road, its shafts and galleries now fallen in and overgrown with whins and hawthorn. He also bought several small bits of land in and around Maybole, others on which part of the village of Crosshill was later built, and two or three farms in the distant parishes of Barr and Ballantrae.

In the very year of his death he was still buying land, and gave a bond for £7,000 for the farm of Threave in Kirkmichael parish. Besides land, his testament mentions furniture, plate, linen, china, and 'wines, spirits, and liquors of all kinds'.

Perhaps, like others who have raised themselves from humble beginnings to wealth and comfort, Niven provoked envy in some of his neighbours. That, I think must have been the foundation of the tradition noted in Mr. Muir's book that 'he became hard and parsimonious to a degree'. For what evidence there is rather points the other way. Niven's testament, for instance, provided generous annuities to his factor and his servants, and in the whole document, the record of which runs to fifteen pages, there is nothing whatever suggestive of a miser. Moreover two writers in the New Statistical Account of Scotland make distinctly friendly allusions to Niven as an improver. One describes the estate of Kirkbride as having been 'a wild, bleak, barren moor' when he first took it in hand, but as so much improved by enclosures, planting, draining, liming, and the erection of 'elegant farm houses' as to give 'the pleasing impression of liberality on the part of the landlord; and domestic comfort on that of the tenant'.[8]

That was written in 1838. In the same year Niven was helping his philanthropic neighbour, Sir Charles Dalrymple Fergusson, who had just succeeded to the estate of Kilkerran, with the expense of building a chapel of ease (since erected into a parish church) for the new weaving village of Crosshill, whose houses had been built on land feued from both Kirkbride and Kilkerran. The implication of these activities is that Niven, far from being parsimonious, was a man of generosity and public spirit. Another favourable account of him appears in a contemporary description of Maybole:

'The town of Maybole has also of late been much improved. Access to it was formerly inconvenient and difficult, but, by the exertions of Mr. Niven of Kirkbride, who has always taken the greatest interest in the improvement of his native place, the streets have been opened by spacious roads to and from all quarters.' [9]

I possess one letter of Niven's which gives a glimpse of his road-making activities a quarter of a century before this time. Written on 28 July 1813, it shows that Niven had been busily promoting the extension of the by-road near Crosshill leading to Baird's Mill, to continue it for a further mile or so till it should join the road to Maybole constructed some twenty-two years earlier along the north-western slope of the Girvan valley: The project involved 190 'falls', four pends, and 'building the bridge and making a pend over the mill lade'. Niven had visited four other neighbouring lairds and fourteen farmers and procured subscriptions from them all, contributing five guineas himself - as much as anybody else except Mr. Thomas Francis Kennedy of Dunure who had put down ten. He had found some contractors, 'people in whom I have confidence', and got an estimate for the work. The sum so far subscribed would meet nearly two-thirds of the cost, and he now sent the estimate and subscription list to old Sir Adam Fergusson of Kilkerran (grand-uncle of the future Sir Charles), a notable improver in his time who had formerly made several miles of road in the Girvan valley. It was apparently he who had suggested the Baird's Mill road, since Niven expressed his hopes of its being completed 'to your satisfaction. ... I trust,' he continued, 'you will not doubt that I used my best exertions,' and he respectfully invited Sir Adam 'to make up the balance'. Sir Adam readily agreed to subscribe twenty guineas, half the balance: it was probably the last of his many contributions to the improvement of his countryside, for he died less than two months later, aged eighty. The rest of the money must have been raised, for the road was duly made and is in use today, though Baird's Mill is now a farm only.

Although he thus 'used his best exertions' as landowner and town councillor, Niven never became a magistrate of Maybole, as did his brother-in-law John Goudie in 1818. But in the first burgh election after the Reform Act, when town councils at last became popularly elected bodies, Niven was returned in a respectably high place on the list of successful candidates, despite having reached the ripe age of seventy-three. He remained on the council for another five years, and attended his last meeting on 14 October 1837. His death came seven years later.

It may be guessed that Niven had had dreams of founding a landed family. In his old age, when he had come to believe that his father, the Maybole shopkeeper, had been styled John Niven of Kirklandhill, he included in his testamentary disposition one clause in which vanity and disappointment are rather touchingly mingled. Any heir succeeding to his lands, he stipulated, must assume and retain 'the name, arms, and designation of Niven of Kirkbride'.

He had, in point of fact, no arms, although he had for many years been using a seal bearing the coat-of-arms of an old Shetland name, Niven of Shousburgh, with which he cannot possibly have had any kinship. He now took steps to obtain arms of his own, and registered them in the Lyon Office on 30 December 1842. They were basically the Shousburgh arms but differenced by 'three spears' heads in pale gules', evidently in allusion to the name of his mother, Janet Spear.

After his death on 13 December 1844, the Kirkbride estate passed to John Goudie, who duly assumed Niven as a middle name, and later to Niven's grand-niece Charlotte Hutcheson, only child of Hugh Hutcheson of Smithfield, Renfrewshire. She had married in 1832 Thomas Montgomery Cunninghame, on his brother's death in 1846 became the eighth baronet of Corsehill and died in 1870. She survived till 1902 as 'the Dowager Lady Charlotte Montgomery Niven Cuninghame',[10] but with her death Niven's name died out. Her grandson, another Sir Thomas Montgomery Cuninghame, sold Kirkbride to its present owners. Niven's portrait, by an unidentified artist, which was long at Kirkbride, was presented by Sir Thomas to the town council of Maybole about forty years ago, and is preserved in the town house. It has lately been cleaned and restored. His house in the High Street remains, appropriately, a bank.

1 *Letters of Robert Burns*, ed. Ferguson, i, pp. 1-4, 39; ii, p. 363.

2 *Robert Burns till his Seventeenth (Kirkoswald) Year*, p. 79.

3 Register of Deeds, vol. 230 (Mack.), f. 115.

4 Register of Deeds, vol. 739, pp. 250-4.

5 Ayr Sasines, xliii, ff. 217, 240, 409.

6 Register of Deeds, vol. 739, p. 253.

7 *Ibid.*, pp. 238-54.

8 *New Statistical Account of Scotland*, Ayrshire, pp. 502-3.

9. *Ibid.*, p. 380.

10 Thus in the Valuation Rolls for Carrick.

7

The Weird of Drummochreen

I

The Ayrshire family of McAlexander of Drummochreen was notorious rather than distinguished. Long though it lasted, it never rose in the world nor increased its small estate. Its head was neither a baron nor a Crown tenant nor even, strictly, a laird, merely the Goodman of Drummochreen, holding his land from a subject-superior. None became even a Justice of the Peace or a Commissioner of Supply. The McAlexanders made their mark in Ayrshire history, none the less, and it was usually a black one. Most of the family was unfortunate; some were scandalous. They seemed to live under a curse. Yet their race was ancient and they kept their identity as a landed family for nearly three hundred years.

There were several McAlexander families in southern Carrick, which all appear to have sprung from a certain Colin McAlexander of Daltippen, a man of considerable substance in the time of King Robert III. Their houses, Daltippen, Pinmore, Corsclayes, Dalreoch, Glenmuck, Drummore and Drummochreen, were dotted about the valleys of Carrick's two rivers, the Girvan and the Stinchar. Frequently renewed kinships united them: they married each other's daughters, witnessed each other's bonds and sasines, and executed each other's testaments.

John McAlexander of Drummochreen, who appears on record in 1498, was probably the third son, named as such in 1479, of Alexander McAlexander of Pinmore and his wife Annabella Colquhoun.[1] I find little about him except that he was before the Court of Justiciary in Ayr in 1511 charged with the theft of a 'bulgeit'- a budget or leather bag.[2] But it was probably he who acquired the forty-shilling land of Drummochreen and built a house in a crook of the Water of Girvan. For some time the name, spelt in countless different ways, had an extra syllable - 'Drummollochryne' - but apart from the prefix 'Drum', meaning a ridge, its corrupted Gaelic is unintelligible.

James Paterson, the county historian, writing in 1847, asserted that of this house 'no remains now exist', but he cannot have looked for any for his words are not true even today. A fragment of wall some twelve feet high, with a window in it, still stands, though less of it than in my youth. The wall, three feet thick, is rough rubble but the well shaped jambs and sill of the window suggest a house of some architectural quality. It was not a castle nor a tower but a stout stone manor-house, set on a small nose of land with the river flowing round three sides of it, a building of quite modest size, perhaps of two storeys but probably comprising only five or six rooms. Its eighteenth-century owners were not assessed for the window tax which was levied only on houses with at least eight windows.

As landowners, the McAlexanders were flanked by the Kennedys of Girvanmains and Drummellan and faced, across the river, by the Fergussons of Kilkerran. The river formed the southern march of their property which, less than a mile wide, slanted up the side of the valley to its skyline, the hill of Craigdow. It did not amount to a thousand acres, but it was a snug little estate, most of it facing south, protected from the prevailing south-west wind, and with the small ridge of Drummochreen sheltering the house if the wind veered to the north. It included some fertile land, plenty of timber, salmon and trout fishing, and a mill further up the river where the current ran strongly through a double bend. Moreover up on the hillside was a valuable seam of coal, worked in those days by shallow burrowings into the surface which the old miners called 'ingaun ees'. The coal-heugh of Drummochreen was just south of the modern farm which keeps the estate's name but was once distinguished from the manor-house as the High Mains of Drummochreen. 'Old shafts' are marked on the six-inch Ordnance Survey map, but although the coal was still being worked in living memory the shafts were filled in a few years ago. A tumbled complex of mounds and hollows, overgrown with ash, thorn and whin, indicates the old spoil-heaps. Beside them runs a meandering burn which further down the hill has cut itself a little glen, steep-sided though hardly fifty feet in depth, called the Captain's Glen - nobody remembers why. The coal-heugh was to figure several times in the family history.

By 1519 John McAlexander had settled Drummochreen on his son James,[3] but the next recorded owner, in 1548, was one George, and after him came Andrew, identified as a brother of the laird of Corsclayes.[4] Andrew McAlexander is first on record in 1570, and nearly thirty years later appears as the first victim in the family's train of misfortunes.

The end of the 16th century was a time of much disturbance in Carrick through the great vendetta carried on between the two leading Kennedy houses of Bargany and Cassillis. Many small families, though not Kennedys, became inescapably involved. Andrew McAlexander, living only three miles up the river from Bargany, might have been expected to side with that powerful chief; but Carrick divisions in the feud were not territorial and Andrew was attached to the interest of the Earl of Cassillis, like all his nearest neighbours including his immediate superior Hew Kennedy of Girvanmains whose strong castle of Dalquharran stood on the Water of Girvan's right bank less than a mile below Drummochreen.

Girvanmains was in his turn a vassal of the Earl's and had a tack from him of the Drummochreen teinds - the Church rents, fallen into secular hands since the Reformation - which he sub-let to Andrew. But the latter, being, says the Kennedy chronicler, 'ane proud man,' sought and obtained from Lord Cassillis a direct tack of the teinds, thus raising himself one step on the feudal ladder. This annoyed Girvanmains. His financial loss in rent was small but the transaction over his head was a slight upon him, and in September 1599 he rode to Cassillis to protest against it.

He was received very coldly. Cassillis took Drummochreen's part. 'Ye dare nocht find fault with him,' he told Girvanmains threateningly, 'for an ye do, we know where ye dwell.' Girvanmains could not vent his wrath on Cassillis, in whose house he was at the moment, but he promised to make Drummochreen sorry for it if he persisted in bypassing him. 'Ye dare nocht steir him, for your craig,' replied Cassillis contemptuously, and turned him out - 'bad him gang to 'his yett.' Girvanmains rode away in a fury.

The old road into the Girvan valley from Maybole crossed the moor of Craigdow above Drummochreen and as Girvanmains followed it he recollected that Drummochreen would be returning home the same way and determined to seize this opportunity for revenge. Posting a boy, William McFedries, as a look-out, he and the two other servants with him concealed themselves behind a knowe till Andrew McAlexander came in sight accompanied by his brother Thomas McAlexander of Corsclayes and Oliver Kennedy of Glenmuck. On young William's signal the three rode out from their hiding-place, spurred after Andrew and 'strak him with swordis on the heid and slew him.' Corsclayes and Glenmuck were either too surprised or too slow to intervene, for 'thai strak never ane straik in his defence.' [5]

Cassillis was 'very far offendit at this deid' but despite his previous warning to Girvanmains he did not venture to test the strength of Dalquharran, but left justice to the ordinary course of law. The murderers were summoned to answer for their deed and not appearing were denounced rebels and put to the horn.[6] Beside the lonely moorland road a cairn was raised to mark the fatal spot, and as 'the cairn of Drummochreen' became a well known landmark. Though somewhat subsided into the rough grass, it is still to be seen.

Andrew McAlexander left a widow, Jonet Kennedy, and 'bairns,' so Thomas McAlexander who succeeded to Drummochreen, and who on 6 November 1599 bought himself a black horse in Ayr for 300 merks,[7] was evidently his eldest son. He enjoyed his inheritance for only a few months, for he had been rashly trying to push his fortunes by engaging in systematic crime. During the seven months when he lay in prison in Edinburgh Castle awaiting trial, and perhaps for the very reason that he was under the deepest suspicion, his father's murderers were allowed to make their peace with the Crown. In 3 January 1601 the escheat of Girvanmains's goods, forfeited on his becoming a rebel, was granted to one John McCluir of Dalquharran, clearly one of his own dependents, and on the sa me day he and his accomplices received a remission under the Privy Seal for 'the slauchtir of umquhile Andro McAlexander of Drummalchrene.' [8] Girvanmains made, no doubt, a friendly arrangement with McCluir and recovered his property.

9. The cairn of Drummochreen

10. The remains of Drummochreen

11. Waulkmill Cottage, Drummochreen

12. Old Dailly Kirkyard

The crime of which Thomas McAlexander, with five others, as accused in May 1601 was making and uttering false coin. In a country so chronically short of bullion that foreign coins were in common circulation the temptation to add to the supply must have been strong, but the law reckoned coining as treason. Against Thomas and his partners the King's Advocate had assembled a formidable and extremely detailed body of evidence. They had evidently formed part of a well organized gang who over a period of some three years had produced quantities of false coins - five pound, four pound and ten shilling pieces besides crowns - in such discreet places as a 'bak chalmer' in Glasgow, and had passed them in Edinburgh and allover the west country from Glasgow to Maybole. There were also charges of burglary.

All six panels were convicted by the jury and all condemned to suffer death on the Castle Hill of Edinburgh. Two, found guilty only of theft, were hanged, but Thomas himself and the others underwent a different form of strangling: they were to be 'wirreit at ane staik quhill they be deid.' The goods of all six were ordered to be escheated to the King.[9]

In Thomas's case there was no question of granting his escheat indulgently to a friend of the family. It was given to Sir Hew Campbell of Loudoun, hereditary Sheriff of Ayr, a distinguished man with a long record of public service, as a suitable present on the day when he was admitted a member of the Privy Council: he was created Lord Campbell of Loudoun a few days later. However he proved kind to the McAlexanders. For a suitable consideration, no doubt, he granted Drummochreen and other lands to Thomas McAlexander of Corsclayes, the coiner's uncle, on whose death in 1603 he confirmed the grant to his son George, the heir. [10]

But Thomas of Drummochreen had left two brothers, John and Andrew, and John was determined to hold on to the family estate and not yield it to his cousin. He simply refused to leave it. His uncle Thomas of Corsclayes had as the new lawful owner taken sasine of Drummochreen on 29 April 1603: in person he arrived on the estate and in the age-old ceremony, continued down to 1845, received, after the reading of his legal title to it, earth and stone of the Drummochreen land from the hands of Lord Loudoun's bailie before witnesses and a notary public. Yet only a month later John Alexander signed a formal contract to supply the Kennedys of Bennan with coal from 'his' coal-heugh.[11] He raised no objection to George's taking sasine of Drummochreen in his turn in November 1604, and in the interval he himself rode over to Corsclayes on the Water of Stinchar to witness George's taking sasine there as his father's heir, a friendly gesture from one cousin to another.[12] But when George tried to turn him out of Drummochreen not merely on paper but in fact he resisted forcibly, as George's subsequent complaint to the Privy Council in 1605 narrated.

A servant of George's, Duncan Gray, was sent to Drummochreen on 28 March 1605 with a formal precept of warning to John to remove himself. It appears that John was not at home so that Duncan must have, in the customary manner, affixed the paper to his door. Soon after his departure John McAlexander 'laip on horsbak' and pursued him 'with all his speid'. He overtook Duncan at Auchenblain and 'with ane grite battoun' struck him many blows on the head and body 'to the effusioun of his blude in grite quantitie,' and 'fellit him thairwith deid to the ground quhair he left him lyand.' This accusation was a little exaggerated since Duncan was not left 'deid'. He survived to assist his master to lay this and another complaint before the Council three years later in January 1608, along with a fellow-servant, John Fergie, whom John McAlexander had assaulted in Ayr on 6 August 1607. John had first abused Fergie 'with mony injurious and contumelious speitcheis', then 'with his fauldit neve gaif him a grite straik upoun the face and left ee quhairof he is liklie to lsse the sicht', and finally drawn his whinger and 'strak diverss straikis at him'. Since John McAlexander failed to appear to answer these complaints he was denounced rebel and put to the horn.[13] This seems to have worried him little: anyhow he held on to Drummochreen.

His brother Andrew sought his fortune in Edinburgh. He married Catherine Annand, a goldsmith's daughter, in 1613 - being described in the marriage register as 'Andrew McAlexander, gentleman' - and in 1616 was admitted a burgess of Edinburgh, having by then become a merchant dealing in hackbuts.[14] He kept in touch with his brother John, and stood caution for him in 1618 when he was again summoned to answer George's charges of thrashing his servants. This time John counter-attacked. He lodged a complaint that he had not been lawfully summoned, and since George did not appear to answer this the Lords suspended John's homing and indeed the whole process.[15] John remained in possession of his estate, and in 1624 formally received from Hew Kennedy of Girvanmains, who had somehow recovered the superiority, a new sasine as the lawful owner of Drummochreen. [16]

The record of John's re-establishment shows the importance of his coal-heugh. He had obviously been working it regularly. In 1603, as already mentioned, and again in 1617,[17] he had contracted to supply coal to the Kennedys of Bennan; and when in 1624 he took the new sasine of his estate he received not merely the statutory earth and stone but also a lump of coal. His son's sasine in 1651, too, was given not at the mansion-house, as was usual, but at the coal-heugh ('apud carbonarium'). [18]

The coal-heugh, a few years earlier, had yielded up something more sinister than coal, bringing a well deserved death to William McAlexander 'in Drummollochren,' who must have been one of the family, though of what kin to John is uncertain. On a November evening of 1620, 'in the twilight' near the coal-heugh, he murdered a neighbour, one Thomas Fergusson, son of the deceased John Fergusson in Ballochneill. Whether they quarrelled there suddenly or whether William had harboured some grudge against Thomas is unknown, but by his own confession he did not kill him in fair fight but struck him 'behind his bak throw the body with ane sword and then feld him with the sword gairdis.' They were close to the farm of High Mains of Drummochreen: it was imperative to hide the body at once. So the murderer dragged it into the coal-heugh and, no doubt, hid it in one of the old workings.

Thomas Fergusson's disappearance apparently caused little concern. His friends thought he had gone to Ireland, which perhaps had been known to be his purpose. But the following June his body suddenly came to light. In a time of heavy rain the burn ran in high spate, overflowed into the heugh and washed out the body into the Captain's Glen. Notwithstanding seven months underground the horrid remains were still recognizable.

It was clear that poor Thomas Fergusson had not gone to Ireland. William McAlexander promptly fled from the district and was naturally suspected. Two months later, on 27 August, he ventured back again and was seized 'within the laird of Girvanmaynis boundis.' Before the Bailie-depute of Carrick he confessed his crime. Commission for his trial was instantly issued and no doubt he paid the penalty. [19]

II

John McAlexander died in September 1638, leaving by his wife, Elizabeth Kennedy, a young son to succeed him, David, born in 1617, who in 1644 married in Edinburgh a girl named Margaret McAlexander, obviously a cousin, and probably the daughter of his uncle Andrew, the merchant of hackbuts.[20] John had survived long enough to sign the National Covenant, probably in March 1638, along with his cousins the lairds of Corsclayes and Dalreoch and their sons and his brother Andrew. The first three all signed by the names of their estates, a common practice until the Act of 1672 forbade it to all but peers and bishops, and John McAlexander wrote his in the old form - 'Drummollochryne'.[21]

Most of the Carrick lairds, and the ministers of Dailly, Girvan, Colmonell and Ballantrae, signed the Covenant, which had enthusiastic support in the south-west. Nothing is recorded of the part the McAlexanders played in the Civil War which followed. But forty years afterwards, when the south-west was again boiling with resistance to the Stewarts' attempts at ecclesiastical domination of Scotland, the Drummochreen family is again on record-and again, as usual, in trouble.

Charles II, soon after his restoration, had issued through the Privy Council a proclamation returning the Church of Scotland to what he called 'its right government by bishops as it was before the late troubles'.[22] Presbyterian ministers who were willing to accept the royal supremacy and episcopal supervision were 'indulged' and allowed to undertake parochial charges; but the bulk of their people abhorred their ministrations and preferred to worship under ministers of their own choice in conventicles, held in private houses (Killochan, near the church of Dailly, was one) or in retired places outdoors. There was an indulged minister in Dailly, Mr Thomas Skinner, a former schoolmaster from Angus, and another, Mr

Claud Hamilton, in Kirkoswald, but they preached to largely empty churches.

Conventicles were forbidden by law under heavy penalties, and Parliament attempted to make landowners responsible for suppressing them. As more and more they became armed assemblies, and the local militia could plainly not be trusted to disperse them, the Government early in 1678 resolved on an extraordinary punitive measure, and sent a large body of troops, shudderingly remembered in after years as 'the Highland Host', to be quartered in the disaffected areas of the south-west.

Various landowners who had resisted signing a bond not to allow conventicles to be held on their lands were arrested and brought before a committee of the Privy Council which sat in Ayr. David McAlexander of Drummochreen was one. He was adjudged guilty of being present at two conventicles, for which he was fined £200, and since one of them had been held on Drummochreen land he was fined another £600 for allowing it, and meanwhile was detained a prisoner in the tolbooth of Ayr.

This was a crippling penalty. Eight hundred pounds was the equivalent of eight years' rent of David's whole estate and the payment of such a sum would have ruined him. He petitioned for remission, undertaking to sign the bond, and ten days later this was allowed to him, Sir John Kennedy of Girvanmains standing cautioner for his 'good behaviour' in future. [23]

He did not however escape other exactions. Troops were quartered in his house as in other parts of Dailly parish which had to find billets for 300 men of Lord Caithness's regiment.[24] The rough soldiers behaved as though they were in occupation of an enemy country, helping themselves to whatever they fancied, and they departed, after a few weeks, loaded with loot. 'When the Highlanders went back, one would have thought they had been at the sacking of some besieged town, by their baggage and luggage .... You would have seen them with loads of bed-clothes, carpets, men's and women's wearing clothes, pots, pans, gridirons, shoes and other furniture, whereof they had pillaged the country.' [25]

If they behaved in the house of Drummochreen as they did elsewhere, David McAlexander lost his silver spoons and anything else of value that he possessed. He was a widower now, his wife having died in 1662.[26] Their son John had married, before 1675, his cousin Anna, daughter of Robert McAlexander of Corsclayes,[27] and lived in the farm of Craigdow over the rim of the valley to the north. John and Anna too had suffered from the presence of the Highland Host, for they had sometimes given refuge to wandering Presbyterian ministers. Their home lay within the parish of Kirkoswald, and Mr Hamilton had busily pointed out to the Host's billeting officer which were the houses of his disaffected parishioners. John McAlexander, 'besides free quarters, was obliged to pay eighty pounds Scots.' [28] The great houses as well as the small suffered exactions. Garrisons of troops, distinct from the Host, were placed in Blairquhan, ten miles up the valley, and in Killochan, the latter one being soon shifted to Bargany.

In the following year, 1679, came the murder of Archbishop Sharp in Fife, the Covenanters' open resistance in arms at Drumclog, and their defeat at Bothwell Brig, which was followed by stern inquisition into the activities of local leaders of disaffection. Twenty Carrick men were particularly sought, including the sons of Blairquhan, Drummellan and Drummochreen.

John, like the others, lay low or flitted from one hiding-place to another. He was prosecuted in his absence for participation in the rebellion and suspicion of having been at Bothwell Brig. His property was forfeited in 1681 and the escheat granted to John, 10th Earl of Glencairn, old David being forced in 1684 to find caution for entering Glencairn to it.[29] Possibly John might have escaped forfeiture if he had appeared before the Privy Council in his own defence, for according to Wodrow no proof was adduced that he had been at Bothwell Brig and 'sentence passed only against absents'. But, perhaps prudently, he did not appear, lost his estate, and, though his forfeiture was rescinded like others in 1690, did not recover possession of it till 1693.[30]

At the Revolution the cloud of oppression lifted. John, perhaps on account of his irregular military experience of ten years earlier, became one of the commissioners of militia for Carrick in March 1689. He was styled 'younger of Drummochreen' then and in 1695, [31] so his father must have lived for some years longer though no mention of him is to be found. The last clear glimpse of David is in October 1684 when he is described as aged 67 'or therby', a good age for those days.[32]

There is preserved a charming description of Drum-mochreen as David must have known it before the troubled years began. It was written by Mr William Abercrombie, the minister who had held the charge of Maybole from 1678 till the Revolution when, like other indulged ministers, he had to flit. He subsequently retired to Edinburgh where, some time after 1695, he wrote a valuable account of Carrick as he had known and plainly loved it. He dwells with particular affection on the 'faire pleasant prospect' of the Water of Girvan and the castles, towers and manor-houses set along its winding course, from Blairquhan where it breaks out of the hills at Straiton down to Ballochtoull (now vanished) at its mouth. His picture bears out the phrase that George Buchanan had used of the river 150 years before - '*multis villis amoenis cingitur*'.

Of Dailly Mr Abercrombie says: 'This parish abounds with gentry and mansion-houses all alongst Girvan which gives a very delightfull prospect to any who from the top of the hills, that guard the same, shall look downe upon that pleasant trough.' It would seem that he had often ridden over the hill from Maybole along the old road past the cairn of Dummochreen on his way, perhaps, to enjoy David McAlexander's hospitality, for his description of Drummochreen is not only detailed but lyrical in its praise - 'a small interest but a most lovely thing, being every way so commodious and convenient for living easily that it is as it were ane abridgement of this countrey, having all the accommodations that are dispersed through it all, comprised within its short and small bounds.'

Mr Abercrombie writes as though reproducing the enthusiasm with which David McAlexander would show a guest his small estate, from the bank of the river, curling out of the ancient woods of oak, birch and hazel to flow past his windows, up to the coal-heugh at the head of the little glen and on to the heather-clad height of Craigdow. 'It has,' says Mr Abercrombie, 'a house not for ostentation but conveniency fit to lodge the owner and his nighbours. It hath gardens, orchards, wood, water, all the fishes that swim in rivers, all sort of cattle, sheep, cows, swine and goat, all sort of fowl wyld and tame, all maner of stone for building. . . and coall, moore, mosse, meadow and marle, a wak myln and corn miln, and all manner of artisans and tradesmen within his bounds, and yet the revenue not above 100 lib. per annum.' [33]

The corn and waulk mill - one for grinding corn, the other for fulling the locally woven woollen cloth - brought in some of the estate's revenue, but the river's current that drove them was a mixed blessing. Just below the mills and the nearby ford the swirling waters constantly gnawed away at the river's right bank, thus gradually changing their course and leaving an increasing stretch of dry ground opposite. Over the years about half an acre of land had thus been transferred from Drummochreen on the right bank to Kilkerran on the left at the place below the ford where, as a later laird of Kilkerran noted, 'the water makes great havock.' David McAlexander gave his rights in the abstracted territory to Alexander Fergusson of Kilkerran in exchange for 'the liberty of casting the dambdyke of his corn and walk miln.'

III

But the pleasant years before the storm passed quickly, and Drummochreen never really prospered again. The McAlexanders had had troubles with their neighbours and had been at variance with the Government. It was now their fate to fall foul of the Church, that Church which in recent years had passed through a great fire and yet was not consumed.

When David McAlexander, in October 1684, gave his age as 67 he was appearing with other people from Dailly before another committee of the Privy Council sitting in Ayr which was inquiring into the activities of rebels. They examined at great length Mr Thomas Skinner, minister of Dailly, all the heritors and many parishioners, who all, with obviously concerted unanimity, denied all knowledge of any rebels within the parish or of the whereabouts of those who were on the run. They would admit only that certain people 'did not attend the ordinances', in other words boycotted the parish church. Mr Skinner himself knew, he said, only the wives of the absent rebels, among whom he mentioned Anna McAlexander. David McAlexander, whom he named as one of his elders, stated that 'he converses not with his sone who is fugative'. The depositions in general indicate a sullen passive resistance - and also a complete deterioration of congregational life. Mr Skinner would not say a word against any of his elders but he admitted that 'a great part of his paroch are ofter absent than present at church' and that though he had been 18 years in his charge he had celebrated the Lord's Supper only once, in the previous month, and that only seven of his congregation had then attended, including no more than three of the elders.[34]

His ostracized and unfruitful ministry must have been truly depressing. The tiny mediaeval church was in a state of decay. Lord Bargany had in 1674 promised the other heritors to rebuild it. But he, one of the Government's stoutest opponents, was for long in prison, and the other heritors were mostly ruined by fines, debts, confiscations and the depredations of the Highland Host. Both church and manse must have mouldered for years without repairs or maintenance, and it may have been almost a relief to Mr Skinner when at the Revolution some men called at his manse and warned him to preach no more in Dailly. He slipped away soon afterwards and Dailly had no minister till, two years later, Mr Patrick Craufurd was inducted after the final establishment of Presbyterianism in Scotland.

Late in 1698 Lord Bargany died, and his son and successor undertook to fulfil his father's pledge to build Dailly a new church. The old one had stood at the extreme southern end of the parish since the parishes of Girvan, centuries before, and Barr, in 1658, had been formed out of its southern half. The new church, all agreed, must be built more conveniently near its present centre. The spot chosen was called Milncavish, on the left bank of the river nearly opposite Dalquharran. Some of the materials of the old church were utilized for the new building. By June 1694 the roof was off the old church and there was 'great abuse made in the church yeard by breaking doun the dyke and bringing in horse and cairts'; but by December 'the new kirk' was a landmark and occupied during the following year. [35] John McAlexander - or Alexander, as he was now called, the family dropping the prefix from this time - had been one of the new elders ordained in 1692, soon after Mr Craufurd's induction, and he now had only a mile to travel, though still having to ford the river, to reach the parish church.

The newly enlarged Kirk Session had a huge task before them, and with Mr Craufurd as their moderator, an earnest and active minister, they set about it with determination. They not only had to furnish their new church - it had no pulpit till 1696 - and revive the continuity of worship and the regular preaching and expounding of the Word: they had to rebuild the whole fabric of spiritual and social life in a community which had become poor and debilitated in more ways than one. They were responsible for primary education, for poor relief, and above all for the people's orderly behaviour and moral welfare; and they were not merely the elected leaders of the community but in law and in fact a court of the Church, their authority both limited and supported by a higher court, the Presbytery of Ayr.

They found a new schoolmaster in 1692 - his predecessor had been arrested as a rebel and hanged in Edinburgh in 1684 - and made him Session Clerk. They instituted an 'extraordinar collection every moneth for the poor in the parish.' And they set themselves to battle against the moral decay which had gripped the neighbourhood, like every community whose standards of conduct have been shaken by war and revolution. It is easier to criticize their severity than to match their zeal.

The Session's first minute-book - all their earlier records had disappeared during the troubles or perhaps been carried off by Mr Skinner - shows that they set up from the start an uncompromisingly strict code of godly, sober and civil behaviour to which they were determined that their people should conform. They disciplined them for swearing, scolding, drunkenness, Sabbath-breaking, drinking in the ale-house in time of sermon, fornication and adultery - and all these things they called by their plain names. Delinquents, either privately persuaded or formally cited by the officer, were summoned before the Session. If found guilty, on either the evidence of at least two witnesses or not infrequently their own confessions, they were rebuked, and exhorted to repentance, sometimes in private, often before the whole congregation. It was thus made clear that social sins were not only against God's laws but injured his people on whose behalf the minister reproved them and held up the shame-faced culprits as a warning to others.

Vice and virtue were unmistakably black and white; and just as the Session felt bound to reckon even the untimely pulling of nuts or replacing of two or three fallen divots on a dyke as Sabbath-breaking, so they were no respecters of persons. Sexual lapses were condoned in nobody. In the first nine years of Mr Craufurd's ministry four even of the heritors appeared before the Session on charges of sexual misconduct: one, who confessed to adultery with his servant-girl, was actually ordered to appear for public rebuke 'in sackcloth every Sabbath day for some space of tyme' - and did so. Nor did the Session hesitate to deal out evenhanded justice to one of their own number, who fell from grace only six months after they had chosen him their representative in the Presbytery of Ayr - John Alexander younger of Drummochreen, to whom an illegitimate daughter, Helen, was born in March 1695.[36]

John's wife Anna was dead by this time, and he had indulged in a liaison with one Jean McKelrath - so the clerk renders the name usually spelt Macilwraith (accented on the first syllable). She confessed her fault to the Session on 7 October 1695 and was rebuked. John was cited to appear at their next meeting.

For a long time he could not face the shame of appearing before the court of which he was a member. He sent excuses to one meeting after another - 'he behooved to be at Air'; 'he was sick'. At last, after six months, he presented himself. On 19 April 1696 'Drummochrein compeired and confessed his sin of fornication with Jean McKelrath, was rebuiked, and suspended from the exercise of the office of ane elder, and ordained to be publicklie rebuiked the nixt Sabbath for the first tyme.'

Jean had been let off with a single public appearance. John had to face the ordeal for three spring Sundays in succession before he was absolved. Thereafter his name occurs no more in the Session's minutes except that on 23 May they allowed him 'ane testificat of his being a single person.' Having evidently decided that it was better, as Paul says, to marry than burn, he went to Edinburgh and there about September espoused a girl from Argyll named Catherine Millan. [37]

The Kirk Session of Dailly were soon concerned again with Drummochreen though not this time with its owner. The coal-heugh at the High Mains was still being worked, probably not by John Alexander himself but by a contractor to whom he would have granted a lease, under the supervision of a grieve named Andrew Kerr. By this time coal could no longer be extracted through 'ingaun ees' and a shaft had been sunk. There was trouble with water in the pit. No proper pumps existed in those days, and perhaps the burn that had once washed out Thomas Fergusson's corpse still occasionally flooded it. The colliers could hardly be blamed for baling out water on a wet July Sunday in 1701; but this was strictly a breach of the ordinance to 'do no manner of work' on the Sabbath day, the only exceptions allowed being 'works of necessity and mercy'. Andrew Kerr was 'spoken to' on the matter in August and on 26 October he and some of his men excused themselves before the Session, 'thinking it was a work of necessity'. The Session quite likely agreed but felt obliged to remit them to the Presbytery for the higher court to decide this difficult point. The Presbytery advised the Session to rebuke the colliers privately - perhaps formally only - 'and take their promise not to do the like again without acquainting the minister and session of the necessity thereof,' a solution which no doubt worked satisfactorily since the matter did not trouble the Session again.

Besides a son by his second wife, born in 1699, John Alexander left at least two sons by his first; David, his heir, and Robert who became a minister and was ordained and inducted to the charge of Girvan in 1712. William, another son or possibly a cousin, became a doctor. This was the most respectable generation of the family.

David Alexander of Drummochreen seems to have led a quiet and orderly life. He married, perhaps in 1716, Jean Kennedy, daughter of Alexander Kennedy of Kilhenzie, and had at least two sons and three daughters. In 1726 we find him present in Dailly at meetings with other heritors and a Presbytery committee to decide on the repair of the manse - indeed a virtual re-building of it - and on one occasion the only heritor to turn up.

The fact that the manse needed so much attention only 30 years after its erection - the new church itself had to be wholly rebuilt in 1766 -

and the obvious seriousness of the decision to expend on the work £187 2s Scots (less than £16 sterling) are evidence, along with contemporary rent-rolls, of how poor even the heritors were at this period. David Alexander borrowed money from his brother the minister which he was never able to repay. In 1721 and 1722 he had gone to great trouble to secure arbitration about an old debt owed to his grandfather by the deceased Hew Kennedy of Bennan: it was worth while to obtain the repayment of so small a sum as 360 merks ,£20 sterling.

The spectacular improvement of Scottish agriculture later in the century was slow to begin in Carrick. There was only one 'improver' in the Girvan valley, and agricultural reform did not develop there in time to save Drummochreen for the family after David died, to be succeeded by his two sons in turn, Robert and John. In all probability the estate never recovered from the exactions and privations it suffered in the 1680s and the long succession of bad harvests just before the Union of 1707.

I have not discovered the date, after 1726, of David's death - the parish registers of Dailly and Kirkoswald are defective at this period - but Robert, born in 1719, must have succeeded to Drummochreen very young, certainly before he was 21. He seems to have early won a reputation for loose conduct, and was noticed to be on much too familiar terms with a servant-girl named Jean Mitchell whose character had 'not stood fair for some years,' the daughter of one of the Drummochreen colliers, William Mitchell. On 19 July 1741 the Kirk Session of Dailly took note of 'a fama clamosa' accusing Robert Alexander of Drummochreen of 'indecent behaviour with the said Jean' and of the names of thirteen people who could bear witness to it.

Robert at first declined to appear before the Session on the plea of illness, next declared that 'he would neither confess nor deny the charge,' and then offered 'a paper of defences' asserting that he 'never was in her company from any bad intention' and that the Session had nothing against him but their own officiousness and suspicion. He threatened to appeal to the Presbytery of Ayr, but in fact did not.

On 6 September the Session decided to delay pursuing the matter 'because of the throng of harvest'; but when they resumed it in

October they found strong evidence against Robert Alexander whose case in the end occupied them for several months. The details, recorded in the neat but tiny handwriting of Mr James Scot the Session Clerk and schoolmaster, throws much incidental light on the simple ways of life in a country parish in early Georgian days.

Jean Mitchell, interrogated on 16 October, 'would not refuse she was with child' and witnesses confirmed her association with Robert Alexander. One testified to having called at William Mitchell's house about a year before, 'and looking over the doorhead, by the light of the fire she observed Drummochreen and Jean Mitchell both in bed ... but did not observe Drummochreen after opening the doors.' Jean was examined again. She 'behaved herself insolently' and told one of the witnesses, an elderly woman, that 'she would take her own time with her'. But at length, on 18 November, she admitted that 'she had been disingenuous' and that Robert Alexander, not an unidentifiable soldier whom she had first accused, was the father of her child.

The minister, Mr William Patoun, wrung a private confession from Robert about a week later but could not induce him to repeat it before the Session till 13 January. Robert may have yielded because Jean's child, Margaret, had been born on the 4th and her baptism was being delayed. She was baptized on the 17th and the Session, who thought the whole affair 'complex', now tried to bring Robert 'to satisfy the publick' in church.

But not even the Presbytery could force Robert to do that. His repentance would go no further. He had promised 'not to haunt the said Jean's company as formerly' but even though interdicted he allegedly still did so and moreover 'in the dead of night'. He was very young, apparently in bad health, fatherless and beset by various worries: Jean's company may have been his only comfort. The Session for their own part were 'willing to show some lenity' towards him but they were under pressure from the Presbytery who considered him contumacious. The unhappy young man's gathering misfortunes during 1742 are partly reflected in his various temporizing excuses which Mr Patoun reported to the Session. He was ill; he had to attend the funeral of his grandmother 'Lady Kilhingie'; he was deeply in debt and 'obliged to abscond, being under horn and caption.'

Early in March he told Mr Patoun that 'such was his situation in the mean time for want of body cloaths that he was ashamed to look out of doors'. But the Presbytery were inexorable, and on 18 April Robert was, by their direction, 'laid under the sentence of the lesser excommunication, and intimation thereof made from the pulpit, for refusing to subject himself to the censures of the Church.' Five months later, on 25 September, he died. He was only 22 years old.

The unfortunate Robert's complaint of being under horning and caption showed that the estate was now heavily burdened with debt and no enviable inheritance for his brother. John indeed soon found himself obliged, early in 1747, to part with the whole property to a neighbouring farmer, Quintin Dick of Auchleffin (now called Lochspouts) who had already bought the farm of Craigdow from Robert in 1740.[38] Thus in the middle of the 18th century Drummochreen at length passed from the McAlexanders who had held it since the 15th.

Quintin Dick did not keep Drummochreen long. He sold it in 1755 to Robert Moore, merchant in Ayr, whose trustees in 1794 sold it to Thomas Kennedy of Dunure whose family had acquired the neighbouring estate of Dalquharran. [39] Thirty years later Kennedy's son sold it to Sir David Hunter Blair of Blairquhan who by now owned also the Drumburle land marching with Drummochreen to the east. [40] From him Sir Charles Dalrymple Fergusson bought both Drummochreen and Drumburle in 1845 since when they have been part of the estate of Kilkerran.

But John Alexander continued to occupy the old house by the river, and soon fell into the same scandals as his late brother. Jean Mitchell had been for some time a servant in the house, and so also had one Sarah Shaw who, like Jean, 'had her residence for some time near the heugh of Drummochreen.' On 3 November 1749 Sarah, now living at the farm of Mains of Thomastoun in the parish of Kirkoswald, gave birth to a child. Interrogated by the Kirk Session of Kirkoswald, she said that her child's father was John Alexander, who 'was guilty with her in the kitchen of Drummochreen about three days after Candlemas last'. John Alexander, summoned before the Kirk Session of Dailly, confessed his guilt, made one public appearance in Dailly church, 'and in regard he is instantly alledged to be going off for the army, he was absolved, seeming penitent', on 17 December 1749.

If John did join the Army he did not stick to it. He was back, or had remained, in Dailly parish two years later when Sarah Shaw, still unmarried, was again pregnant and thought it best to leave the district. Various witnesses later remembered that her intimacy with John Alexander had been renewed, and reported her story that he had advised her to go away and had given her ten shillings for her journey. Sarah herself said 'that Drummochreen and she parted when she was leaving the country at the Kairn of Drummochreen', that memorial of the murder of John's ancestor 150 years before. It sounds as if he had seen her off on her journey, accompanying her to the spot where the road opens up a wide view of the country to the north and Girvan valley is at length left behind.

In 1754 John married, but his wife can have brought no great tocher with her to revive the family's declining fortunes. She was the daughter, named Janet, of a farmer, Quintin Black, 'portioner of Meikle Brockloch', and bore him a son who was called David. Then, towards the end of 1757, Sarah Shaw appeared in Dailly, and was questioned about her second child. She affirmed that it was alive and had been baptized 'by a young minister ... without any sponsor', but that she had had no fixed residence since she went away and had never been 'judicially conveened before any kirk session'. John Alexander of Drummochreen, she said, had been the father of this child too.

The Kirk Session of Dailly thought her story 'pretty singular' and investigated it almost as fully as they had formerly done Robert Alexander's affair with Jean Mitchell. Their moderator was now Mr Thomas Thomson who, having been chaplain in the Kilkerran family, had become minister of Dailly after Mr Patoun's death in 1755. He had a private talk with John who as a result 'offered a voluntary attendance on the Session' but denied being responsible for Sarah's second baby. His first statement averred that he had not even spoken to her since her first child was weaned; but he later amended it, 'as it would be absurd to imagine he would not speak with her did he meet her with his child in her arms, or not ask how his child was if he was passing by her door'. One witness indeed had 'observed Drummochreen and the said Sarah meeting in the hill, the little child being in her arms, but depones she never saw any indecent behaviour'. John persisted in his denial and claimed the benefit of an Act of Assembly restricting prosecution for such offences within a period of five years; and on Mr Thomson's advice the Session, on 18 March 1759, dropped the case.

Like his brother, John Alexander did not live long, though he was nearly thirty-eight when he died in February 1760. Their father had not apparently lived to be old, and the early deaths of both brothers suggests the possibility of some persistent ailment in the family.

Janet, John's widow, married again, her second husband being evidently a cousin of her first, Thomas Alexander, merchant in Maybole. This kinsman had been appointed tutor and curator to little David, whose inheritance consisted only of debts, apart from a one-third share of a legacy of £1,000 from his great-uncle the former minister of Girvan. [41] His life, like his father's and uncle's, was probably short, for it was his half -brother Robert, the Maybole merchant's son, who was served heir-general to their mother in 1804.

IV

Thereafter the family fades out of history though various descendants loom dimly in the mists. There were and still are many Alexanders in Carrick, and among them there evidently grew up a quite baseless legend that Drummochreen had not really been alienated and that some vaguely valuable heritage still attached to its name. One Alexander after another took up this shadowy claim, such as a John Alexander, excise officer in Maybole, and a Quintin Alexander, planter in Jamaica, who both styled themselves 'of Drummochreen' and must have been cadets of the family. Much more dubious pretenders were two Irishmen, William Mark, of Markston, Ireland, and John McVie, of Tullygrully, Ireland, who got themselves served heirs-portioners to this John and Quintin in 1804 and 1809, claiming to be their cousins. [42]

James Paterson tells a story specifically linked with these Irish claimants. They were, a correspondent told him, relations of one John Shaw, a poor old beggar in Ireland who wandered about with a 'show-box' or peep-show and alleged himself to be the rightful heir to a valuable estate in Scotland. Though laughed at for his pretensions, he made several wills bequeathing his rights to a lady who had been kind to him and in whose house he at length died. He claimed to be lawfully descended from a laird of Drummochreen's sister who had eloped with a weaver to Ireland.[43] But his name indicates that he must have been the offspring of poor Sarah Shaw - of whose existence Paterson did not know - brought up to believe in a romanticized version of his illegitimate ancestry.

The family that lived for so long in old Drummochreen and sank through disasters to disgrace is forgotten now, like so many others of the same quality - small heritors, 'mean gentlemen', bonnet-lairds - once so numerous. They played their part in the rural life of Scotland before the agricultural revolution, but one by one their little possessions mostly became absorbed in more progressive estates of more economic size. Unless they were intelligent or active enough to mend their fortunes, only sparse allusions to them, if any, occur in the county histories and they probably drifted away from their native districts or remained only as tenant farmers. Yet, as this reconstructed narrative may show, local and even national history may be illustrated from their not uneventful annals.

Around the surviving fragment of the old house by the river a wandering McAlexander ghost would recognize little today but the unchanging outline of the hills to the south and east. The pleasant gardens and orchards have long ago vanished without trace, though a few old beeches and one great oak were perhaps there as saplings in the last John Alexander's time. All sign of the waulkmill has gone though the miller's cottage was inhabited till a few years ago and still stands, a melancholy shell. Even the river has changed its course below the ford, for early in the nineteenth century the lairds of Kilkerran and Dunure co-operated to straighten its winding banks and so reduce the frequent flooding of the fields which their forebears had improved. It now flows some yards away from Drummochreen instead of under its walls. The riverside fields themselves, some dotted with grazing Ayrshire cows, others golden with oats or barley, now stretch level and wide where in Mr Abercrombie's day the valley floor was 'so covered with wood that it looks lyke a forrest'. Only a patch of that ancient natural forest, some three or four acres in extent, now survives, beyond the river opposite the site of the waulkmill. The rest has vanished as completely as the McAlexanders.

1 *Acta Dominorum Concilii*, ii. p. 283; Register House Charters, 486.

2 Justiciary records: Court Books, old series, ii. f. 148.

3 *Protocol Book of Gavin Ros*. No. 316. See pedigree on p.138

4 Protocol Book of Henry Prestoun. f. 25; Edinburgh Testaments, 15 July 1590.

5 *Historie of the Kennedyis*, pp 29-30.

6 *Register of the Privy Council*, 1st series, vi. p. 622.

7 Register of Deeds, lxxv. ff. 35-6.

8 R.S.S. lxxi. 3 Jan. 1601.

9 Robert Pitcairn: *Criminal Trials in Scotland*, ii. pp. 353-6.

10 R.S.S. lxxii, 8 July 1601; Sec. Reg. Sasines, Ayr, ii. ff. 182-3, 490-1.

11 Sec. Reg. Sasines, Ayr, ii. ff: 182-3; Register of Deeds, clxx. ff. 29-30.

12 Sec. Reg. Sasines, Ayr, ii. If. 403-4, 490-1.

13 R.P.C., 1st series, viii. pp. 38-9.

14 *Edinburgh Marriage Register, Edinburgh Burgess Roll*.

15 R.P.C. xi. pp. 402, 414.

16 Ayr Sasines, iii. ff. 171-2.

17 Paterson, *History of Ayrshire*, i. p. 393.

18 Ayr Sasines, viii. ff. 349-50.

19 R.P.C. (1), xii, p. 568.

20 Edinburgh Marriage Register.

21 *Ayrshire Archaeological Society Collections*, 2nd series, iii. pp. 114-8.

22 R.P.C. (3), i. pp. 28-9, 30-2.

23 *Ibid.*, v. pp. 548, 551, 552, 562, 567.

24 Robert Wodrow: *History of the Sufferings of the Church of Scotland*, i.   p. 494..

25 *Ibid.*, pp. 480, 491.

26 Glasgow Testaments, 18 May 1666.

27 Kennedy of Bennan MSS (Register House), 82-3.

28 Wodrow, ii. p. 162.

29 R.P.C. (3), viii. p. 235; ix. p. 209.

30 Wodrow, ii. p. 162; *A.P.S.* ix. p. 165.

31 *A.P.S.* ix. p. 28; Dailly Kirk Session minutes.

32 *R.P.C.* (8), ix. p. 584. See pedigree on p.138.

33 Macfarlane's Geographical Collections, ii. pp. 10-12, 20.

34 R.P.C. (8), ix. pp. 531-6.

35 Dailly Kirk Session minutes.

36 Kirkoswald parish register.

37 Proclamation 23 August 1696 (Edinburgh Marriage Register).

38 Ayr Sasines, xi. f. 221.

39 *Ibid.,* cvi. f. 63.

40 Gen. Reg. of Sasines, 1611, f. 269.

41 Glasgow Testaments, 24 March 1766; *Services of Heirs Index*, 1760-9.

42 *Services of Heirs Index*, 1800-9.

43 Paterson, i. p. 594, note.

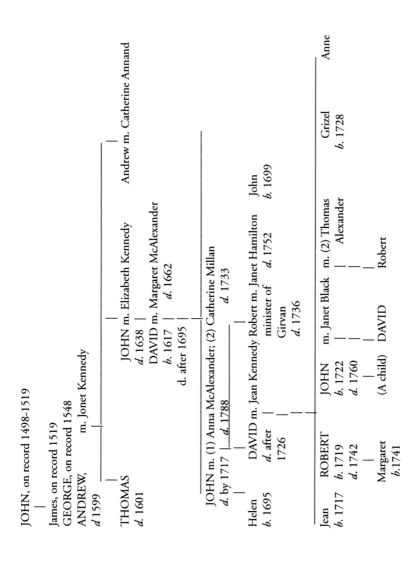

8

Simple Annals

The collector of graveyard inscriptions will find Scotland rather a barren field. Lapidary verse is rare, eulogy of the deceased is generally rare before the nineteenth century, and the instances commonly quoted of unintentionally comic or incongruous inscriptions seldom come from a Scottish source. Nor, in what used to be a poor country, are instances common in our kirkyards of splendid carving, armorial or otherwise: such as exist are mostly indoors, gracing a heritor's aisle.

Thus in Scottish kirkyards the searcher is generally a genealogist. Yet there is much more than genealogy to be found in a kirkyard, and its epitaphs, cumulatively, can throw a suggestive light on our forefathers' way of life.

It took me, in intermittent visits, some twelve years to transcribe and list the inscriptions in the old kirkyard of my native parish of Dailly, which lies in the heart of Carrick in the valley carved out by the Water of Girvan. Old it can be called only by comparison with the present cemetery opened towards the end of Queen Victoria's reign. The original church on this site, replacing in 'a more centrical situation' the mediaeval church at the southern end of the parish, dated only from 1695, and in its kirkyard, now long closed for burials, the oldest inscription is of 1704.

Nine years earlier the roof had been taken off the little mediaeval church at Old Dailly when William, 3rd Lord Bargany, had completed, in fulfilment of an undertaking by his father, the new church at a place then called Milncavish. The little 'kirktoun' around the old church dwindled away and in course of time a village grew up round the new one. Today it is of a good size, increasing rapidly in the present century as many small farms of uneconomic size passed out of existence and the pressure of government and local authority grouped the population where transport, sanitary and social services can most easily be concentrated. The parish is still large, some eight miles long, but the mass of the congregation - miners, farmworkers, small merchants and tradesmen - live within half a mile of the church.

It is not however Lord Bargany's church, which decayed within half a century. The present one, much more solidly built in 1766 and restored, perhaps rather too thoroughly, in 1914-1915, is a comely T-shaped building with large sashed windows, high-pitched slated roof and white-harled walls, its three gable-ends each crowned with a classical urn. The principal feature is a charming square tower in a kind of rustic Renaissance style, with the belfry door set in a blind arch.

The kirkyard once lay all round the church, but in late Victorian times when the main village street was extended over it close past the tower the stones on the north side were removed and set round the outside of the church walls. Further to the north lies the river, on whose bank, a little to the east, stands the manse, rebuilt in 1803, and beyond on the far bank broods the old castle of Dalquharran, ruined these 180 years and shrouded in the trees fast obscuring what were once its policies. The views across the broad valley are closed in by rising hills barred with plantations and dotted with white farm-houses.

The kirkyard has not always been well kept and its rough coarse grass is very different from the smooth turf of the modern cemetery. There are a few recumbent slabs and several large table-tombs, but most of the memorials are upright stones, irregularly aligned and almost all faced eastwards to preserve the inscriptions from the assaults of the weather that blows up the valley from the Irish Sea. Despite this precaution the local sandstone wears badly and many epitaphs are defective and some almost totally erased. The best conditions of light for copying the words, with sunshine sloping at the right angle to show up weathered letters, pass quickly and do not occur daily, and there were many delays and interruptions before I could feel that I had captured every decipherable inscription. Even during those years many deteriorated further, the great frost of early 1963 doing serious damage, and while some epitaphs were caught just in time I lost parts of others which might have been saved only a few years earlier.

Of the names recorded here none is notably predominating. Indeed the variety of names indicates that Dailly people mingled freely with their neighbours and often married outwith the parish boundaries, having easy communications up and down the valley and even over the hills. There are seven names that occur ten times or more: Alexander, Bryden, Dick, Kennedy, McConnell, McGill and Reucassel. Seven others occur more than five times: Blane or McBlane, Hutchison, McIlwrath, McMurtrie, McWhinnie, Scobie and Scott.

Excepting Bryden, Dick, Scobie and Scott, these are all old Carrick or Galloway names or forms of names. So also are some that occur only infrequently: Drynan, McCaa, McFedries, McGarva, McKergow, McKissock, McMyne, McQuater, McQuattie and Wiggam (Wighame).

But among the unique names are a few that seem foreign not only to Carrick but to Scotland - Beaumont, Byrne, Earl, Hervey and Vernon - and are nearly all names of wives, though Christopher Byrne 'from the county of Lowth in Ireland' was a manservant at the modern house of Dalquharran. The fact that he is the only Irishman buried here shows that Irish immigration into Galloway, which intensified in the 1840s, did not then reach as far north as Carrick.

The old names from Galloway, such as McKergow and McQuattie, are a reminder that in the Middle Ages Carrick was a part of that ancient province in which the native language was Gaelic. Even in Carrick that tongue still lingered in the mid-sixteenth century, and it has left its traces, generally much corrupted, all over the local map. Hence about a third of the names on our tombstones begin with 'Mac', of which only two, Mackenzie and Maclean, are obviously not Galloway but Highland.

There are also a few names - Awles, Brim, Coid, Dunshee, McWherror and Muekle - which are not to be found in George F. Black's monumental work *The Surnames of Scotland*, and are probably renderings corrupted.

My record preserves some names and some dates probably traceable nowhere else; but they, I feel, are not all that it has to tell.

It pictures a community, indicates its much wider diffusion over the countryside than today, and tells something of its occupations, interests and hazards.

Farming and mining were the traditional occupations. There is good land in the valley - more of it since the 'improvers' of the eighteenth century drained and cleared the low ground - and a small coalfield, a detached fragment of the great Ayrshire one, whose pits or 'pottis' were valued by the monks of Crossraguel Abbey as far back as the early fifteenth century. The parish in old days had six principal heritors: the lairds of Bargany (Hamilton), Dalquharran (Kennedy), Kilkerran (Fergusson), Killochan (Cathcart), Drummochreen (McAlexander) and Penkill (Boyd). Most of these had their family burying places at old Dailly. Only the Kilkerran one is in the present kirkyard: whatever lair my family had at the old church fell to ruin and disappeared during a long period of misfortune in the seventeenth century. Ours alone, therefore, comparatively modern, stands prominent in the middle of the kirkyard, a high rectangular mausoleum with a peaked roof, simple but well proportioned, very solidly built of finely hewn stone. It is referred to as 'the aisle' in 1778,[1] and was evidently erected by Sir Adam Fergusson over the grave of his father, Lord Kilkerran the judge, who was buried here in January 1759. Nine of the family lie within the vault and five others are commemorated by tablets on the church walls.

The only gravestone embellished with a coat-of-arms perhaps covers the grave of a Kennedy of Drummellan, Alexander, whose family in the reign of George II sold off the last of their lands in Dailly parish.

But if most of the local lairds are not buried here many of their dependents are, whose epitaphs emphasize how much employment in the eighteenth and nineteenth centuries was given by the large estates which till fairly recently made up most of the parish territory. Many of the dead whose calling is unrecorded must have been their labourers, foresters, shepherds, masons, dykers, carters and so forth. Five are specifically named as gardeners, three as estate joiners, and seven as domestic servants. All the latter with one exception have epitaphs of grateful commemoration, and one was mourned in two households, 'Mrs Charlotte Robison, who died ... January 1855 aged 94 years, having been a faithful servant in the Kilkerran and Bargeny families for more than half a century'.

One table-tomb was placed in the kirkyard by a certain John Henry who was employed by Sir Adam Fergusson, first as a surveyor and later as factor, for more than forty years. His bold clear handwriting, apparently modelled on his employer's, is very familiar to me. Mr Henry had a lonely old age. His wife died in 1799, their three daughters, all in their twenties, during the next eight years, but he himself lived on till 1835, dying at the age of eighty-six, when his own epitaph was added to the earlier inscription: 'And now rests here along with his family the said John Henry ... having found from the experience of a long life that here is not our rest'.

Professions or trades are not always specified, but principal among the former are five ministers of the parish and two schoolmasters. All five ministers died in the charge. They are Mr William Steel (1723); Mr William Patoun (1755), commemorated by a mural tablet on the south gable, who married Alexander Kennedy of Drummellan's daughter and was 'a Person equally esteemed for his Abilities as a Public Teacher and for the Virtues of his Private Life'; Mr Thomas Thomson (1798); Mr Charles Cunningham (1815), 'whose kind and warm affections greatly endeared him to his parishioners and friends'; and Mr David Strong (1855), 'possessed of rare meekness, sincerity and patience in well doing.' Mr Strong's successor, Dr George Turnbull, who died in the charge in 1908, is not buried here but is commemorated by a tablet and the iron gates and railings of the kirkyard.

Mr Thomson and Dr Turnbull were outstanding figures, the one ministering here for 42 years, the other for 39. Dr Turnbull gradually led his flock into modern ways of worship, the use of hymns as well as psalms and paraphrases, and of a harmonium (replaced by an organ in 1920), the practice of standing for praise and sitting for prayer instead of the other way round, and that of 'simultaneous Communion' in place of successive 'tables'. He was the last minister in whose time delinquents were summoned to appear for discipline before the Kirk Session. Interested in the history of his parish, he wrote much about it and its traditions, and it was he who instituted the annual memorial service still held at Old Dailly each July near the graves of the parish's martyrs of Covenanting times.

More than a century before Dr Turnbull's induction, Mr Thomas Thomson began his career in my family as chaplain to Lord Kilkerran, combining that office, as often happened in those days, with that of tutor to the judge's numerous children.

It was complicated but not difficult to reward him with the charge of Dailly after Mr Patoun's death. Lord Kilkerran recommended him to the other heritors, who approved, the heritors to the Kirk Session, who likewise approved, and the heritors and Session to the heads of families in the congregation, who approved also, every group unanimously. A petition was then sent to the Crown as patron, and Mr Thomson was duly appointed by a warrant superscribed by King George II's own hand. Such was a normal procedure in the old days of patronage, a principal cause of the many rifts suffered by the Church of Scotland. It was abolished in 1874, and Dr Turnbull was the last minister of Dailly presented by the Crown. It was at least more expeditious than today's democratic procedure in which every member of the congregation has a voice.

Mr Thomson married twice. His first wife - 'the amiable Lucinda' as he called her in their courting days - was a young lady, Peggy Hope, whose family, the Hopes of Kerse, had fallen on evil days and who had found a home with the Cathcarts of Killochan. She did not live long: her gravestone is in the kirkyard, designating her in a formal, old-fashioned way 'Mrs Margaret Hope.' After seven years of solitude Mr Thomson married a widow who bore him a large family, including two famous sons. One was Thomas Thomson, who became the greatest record scholar Scotland ever produced and will be the subject of the next essay of this book. His brother John, who entered the ministry and for five years held the charge of Dailly in succession to his father, won fame as 'Thomson of Duddingston', the first great landscape painter among Scottish artists. His early work was done in the Girvan valley and several examples of it are still in the parish.

Mr Thomson wrote the admirable description of the parish of Dailly in the *Statistical Account of Scotland*. The church, he recorded, was rebuilt in 1766, and according to local tradition he helped with his own hands in the demolition of its predecessor. His account pays tribute to Dailly's standard of education - 'There is scarcely an individual who has not been taught to read and write English.' [2]

For this literacy the credit belongs largely to two schoolmasters buried here. Mr James Scot served the people of Dailly as session clerk for 20 years and as dominie for 35. He must have been an extremely active man for he also held for some years the farm of Moorston whose laird, Sir Adam Fergusson, was a notable 'improver' and did not tolerate slack or backward tenants. On Mr Scot's death in 1775 'his sorrowing school' put an elegant Latin inscription on the seven-foot stone slab that covers his grave. Perhaps a century later its bold lettering was so much weathered that someone carefully recut such parts of it as he could read, but being no Latinist made a sad hash of it.

Better cut and well preserved is the epitaph of Mr James Welsh, schoolmaster from 1780 till his death in 1817. On a total income of some £30 a year this excellent man taught English, Latin, French, writing, arithmetic and book-keeping. To him the two brilliant Thomson brothers owed their early education, and he is buried near their father.

No other professional men are recorded as buried here except one Mr William Robertson who seems, though part of his epitaph is lost, to have been chaplain to Sir John Fergusson, Sir Adam's grandfather, and Alexander Blair who died in 1862 having been 'for many years doctor for the parish of Dailly'. There are two merchants, an innkeeper, two smiths, a miller and a tailor; and the octogenarian Andrew McFedries, buried in 1805, is noted in the parish register to have been a shoemaker.

A great many of the dead must have worked in the local pits, but only one man is specifically described as 'collier', on the only memorial that has become celebrated outside the parish. The ordeal of 'John Brown, collier,' deserves recalling. [3]

On 8 October 1835, in the Kilgrammie pit a mile above the village, the roof of a great part of the workings fell in from a 'crush' caused by the gradual reduction of the retaining pillars of stone and coal beyond the margin of safety. The colliers had noticed indications of a 'crush' for the preceding two days, but with a mixture of recklessness and fatalism had continued work in the threatened area. When at last the huge weight of rock settled down, with a shock and rumble like an earthquake's that were felt a mile or two away and sent the ponies at the pit-head galloping in alarm down to the village, most of the miners escaped through an old day-level which drained the pit. But John Brown, a veteran of 66, insisted on going back to rescue his new jacket, and a final fall of the roof imprisoned him.

As soon as work could be resumed the men made a determined effort to reach John Brown's body. They had no hope of his survival, but one of the ancient superstitions of their craft forbade ordinary work while a 'corp' lay in the pit. For many days they toiled to cut a tunnel through the masses of fallen rock.

But Brown was alive and unhurt, quite without food but, until he grew too weak to stir, able to drink the water that trickled near him. For three weeks he never lost hope of deliverance, from faith in God and trust in his comrades whom he could at length hear tunnelling their way towards him through the rock, the darkness, and the foul air. But at times, as he grew weaker and weaker, his mind wandered; in his dreams he was convinced that the sister of 'the maister', the lessee of the pit, often visited him to cheer him in his living tomb.

At last, on 31 October, the twenty-third day after the disaster, the rescuers broke through into an open working and heard a faint groan ahead of them. Was it devil or man? One of the men solemnly called, 'If that's your ain groan, John Brown, in the name o' God gie anither.' A responding groan encouraged their advance, and groping forward - for the air was too foul to light their lamps - they at length touched the ice-cold body of Brown. 'Gie me a drink,' he whispered, and when they had got him some water continued, 'Eh, boys, but ye've been lang o' coming.'

While the news was carried back to the outer world and preparations were being made to get Brown out through the tunnel, some of his mates stripped and in turn laid their naked backs against his to try to warm him. They brought in some milk for him, and at length, with great

13.Dailly Kirk

14. The Collier's Oak

15. Killochan

16. Old Dalquharran Castle

difficulty, dragging him along on a plank, they got him to the shaft and the cage, where 'the maister' held him in his arms as they ascended. He was a fearful sight as the growing daylight revealed him, not merely reduced to a skeleton but covered with the yellowish-white fungus that infested the rotten timbers below ground. 'Wad ye kittle me?' he asked feebly as 'the maister' tried to pick the fibres out of his beard.

They carried him gently home and laid him in his own bed. The minister, Dr Hill, came. Brown asked him to put up a prayer, and took his hand and thanked him when it was ended. The doctor came, examined him and gave careful directions for his treatment. He was so thin that his vertebrae could be felt through his stomach, his beard was long and glossy, his skin like parchment, and in his skull-like countenance his sunken eyes gleamed with an unearthly brightness. But he was alive, and able to tell at least a part of his tale.

For a day or two he seemed to rally. 'Ah, boys,' he said on Sunday afternoon, 3 November, 'when I win through this, I've a queer story to tell ye.' But the life that had flickered up was already fading, and he died quietly that evening. Three doctors held a post-mortem and found almost all the organs quite sound but the heart 'small and flabby' and the omentum almost wholly absorbed. Their examination did not satisfy some of the older miners who, well used to the activities of the Prince of Darkness underground, could not quite believe that the ghastly thing rescued from the Kilgrammie pit was really their old comrade John Brown. 'Did ye fin' his feet?' they asked Dr Sloan, of Ayr, as he left the cottage, and when the doctor admitted he had not looked at them to make sure that neither was a cloven hoof they went away shaking grave and knowing heads.

They buried John Brown by the south wall of the kirkyard and gave him a fine big tombstone, to the cleaning of which the Dailly miners have contributed more than once since then, with a long epitaph on it composed by Dr Hill.

But it was the open fields rather than the dark galleries underground that provided most Dailly folk with their livelihood. Eight of the men buried in the kirkyard are named as farmers. The earliest, whose stone is dated 1737, is 'John Wilson, late in Maxwelstoun, an eminent

Farmer of severe probity,' who must have developed this impressive character early in life since he was only 47 when he died. Young too was Oliver Lamb, late farmer in Blackbyres, whose 'private worth and public usefulness' led 'a numerous acquaintance, who appreciated his merits and sincerely lamented his premature death,' to erect to his memory a nine-foot obelisk, topped with an urn, in 1838. But David Crawford, farmer in Burnton, reached the age of 84 before his death in 1776, and his grandson John, farmer in Aird, was 90 when he died in 1860.

Dailly, wrote Mr Thomson, had produced 'no very extraordinary instance of longevity', but he had forgotten the death, in 1786, of one Kathrine McCutchion who had outlived her husband John McGill by 48 years and reached the notable age of 104. Where ages are recorded, however, it is not longevity but the pitiful youthfulness of many of the dead that stirs the reader's emotion, reminding him of the appalling hazards that threatened 18th and 19th century childhood. John Reucassel and his wife put up a stone to 'ther 5 children' in 1729 when the father, who himself died on 12 January 1730, was only 42. Four inscriptions record the death of two children together and one of three together, suggesting the ravages of an epidemic in a close-packed but-and-ben; and another tells of an even sadder loss - 'Erected by Hugh Mcrath in memory of his two sons and wife who died Feb. 7, 1821.' Isabella Muir in 1835 lost her five-year-old son in March and her husband Alexander McCall in April, and they had previously buried 'their 3 Infant Children'.

All these sorrowful records, like most of the epitaphs, are brief and factual - 'Here lyes the Corps of John & Francis Howie Both children 1750' - but in another case reticence is poignantly broken by three words:

'Erected to the memory of Gilbert Macilwrath the only child of John Macilwrath and Agnes Niven his mournful parents. He died Octr 26 1762 aged 13.'

Perhaps the most melancholy stone in the whole kirkyard is the innkeeper's. Samuel White, landlord of the Greenhead Inn, who died in 1840, and his wife Jane Mackie had eleven children who all died between the ages of 16 and 36. There may have been some hereditary ailment among them, for their epitaph, after recording the deaths and the ages of the entire family, concludes with the text from Revelations, 'And there shall be no more curse.'

'*Memento mori*' begins the oldest of all the inscriptions, that of James Wiggam who died on 24 August 1704, and his stone is one of eight which bear carved on the reverse side the grim tokens of hour-glass, cross-bones and skull. The latest of these is dated 1743, and all eight stand along the east side of the kirk-yard, clearly the first part of it to be used. One, graced with pilasters and a pediment, includes along with the emblems of mortality a set-square and compasses, and has on the obverse side almost the only specimen of mortuary verse, in memory of Cornelius Campbell and his wife Ann Davidson. They too were perhaps victims of some contagious illness, for, like three other married couples, they died within three days of each other, in July 1735, and were thus commemorated:

> *Here lyes the Husband and the Wife*
> *Who lived a short suet Christian life*
> *Whom death unto the dust did fix*
> *He thirty one she Tuintie six.*

But the stone that says most in fewest words to warn the reader to remember his own latter end is one near the kirk-yard's main gate with the words now only just decipherable, commemorating one John Stevenson, his wife and children, and concluding:

> *Life   Eternity*
> *how short   how long*
>   *1757*

Pious sentiments occur fairly often among the Victorian inscriptions but they are exceptional among the earlier ones. Indeed when the survivors did depart from strictly factual record they were concerned chiefly with their own right of property in the 'lair' which, though not an absolute title, is by the law of Scotland a right in perpetuity to make use of it for sepulture. There is a strong note of insistence on this right in some of the oldest inscriptions. No less than 16 begin with the words 'This is the burial place of - ' and three with 'This stone belongs to - '. Four brothers named Blair, about the middle of the 18th century, placed a stone 'in memory of their Parents and to perpetuate their burying ground', a duty which they clearly considered more urgent than to record their parent's names. In three other cases the owner of the lair carefully stipulated its measurements, such as '4 graves breadth'.

Not everyone however bought a lair, and many buried here have no memorial beyond the parish register which is extant only from 1780. A hundred years ago the grave-digger, according to the recollection of an old man who died in my youth, used regularly to turn up anonymous skulls and bones whenever he dug a new grave in an apparently empty space. He would arrange them in a neat row till he had finished his task and then carefully bury them again. There must thus have been many unmarked graves; a few have been indicated by uninscribed and even unshaped stones. A tradition attaches to one of these, a rough lump of conglomerate rock, which is reputed to have fallen on and killed a worker in the limestone quarry, disused since the 1860s, three miles away on Blair hill. His mates, it is said, carried the fatal stone down to the village and set it over his grave.

Quarrymen, like miners, perhaps had their traditional superstitions. They may have reckoned that a rock which had killed a man was better out of the quarry and set down in the precincts of the church.

1 Dr George Turnbull: *A South Ayrshire Parish*, p. 86. The reference, the source of which I have not traced, is clearly to the mausoleum, 'aisle' being the customary word for a heritor's burial-place, but was misunderstood by Dr Turnbull.

2 *Statistical Account of Scotland*, vol. x. p. 53.

3 *New Statistical Account of Scotland*, v. (Ayr) pp. 392-3; Sir Archibald Geikie: *Geological Sketches*, pp. 70--83.

9

Dailly Church

The Church of 1766

The first church on the present site was built by William, 3rd Lord Bargany, in 1695, in fulfilment of an undertaking by his father. The site was on Bargany estate, and was chosen as being more conveniently central in the parish than the old mediaeval church of which the ruin stands at Old Dailly.

The 1695 church soon proved too small and, it appears, was not very soundly constructed. In 1763 the Heritors - the local landowners who until the present century were responsible for the upkeep of all church buildings - and the Presbytery of Ayr appointed six local tradesmen to examine the church, and they unanimously reported that it was 'altogether in a bad state and cannot be repaired'.

The Heritors of those days were the lairds of Bargany, Kilkerran, Dalquharran, Killochan and Penkill. Unfortunately, the official record of their meetings at that time is lost, and our Kirk Session records say nothing of the rebuilding project. But it seems that the initiative came from the minister, Mr. Thomas Thomson, who had been inducted in 1756 after having been chaplain in the Kilkerran family. He is said to have helped with his own hands in the demolition of the old church, and he recorded later that the new one cost the Heritors £600 - the equivalent of perhaps £ 10,000 in modern money.

The church in 1766 had, as it has today, three lofts, but as built they almost touched each other at the corners. Here the Heritors had their own pews. Lord Bargany's coat-of-arms on the front of the Bargany loft still commemorates the builder of the 1695 church. Each loft was reached by an outside 'fore-stair' and had a small private room with a fireplace behind the pews. The Kilkerran private room was taken out in 1878 to allow more seating in the loft, and the Bargany one adapted about 1893 for use as a vestry.

The new church was much more solidly built than the former one, but as the years went by it too proved unsatisfactory. The ceiling, low above the lofts, made it stuffy. In 1876 the Session recorded that it was 'damp, cold and uncomfortable, especially in winter' and the Heritors considered building an entirely new church. In 1881 they decided to do so and engaged an architect, but they could not agree on a design. Moreover the minister, Mr. Turnbull, objected that the congregation would be without any church during the whole rebuilding, and Sir James Fergusson, then absent in India, threatened to interdict the other Heritors from pulling the old church down. The rebuilding project was therefore dropped.

Certain improvements were made - a new pulpit in 1893 and 12 standard lamps, fed by oil, in 1894, when there also was erected 'a plain press in the Bargany room to hold the Minister's robes'. In 1902 the Heritors considered employing an architect to improve the church, but contented themselves with various repairs. Finally, however, in 1913 they resolved on a complete scheme of restoration, and engaged an eminent Glasgow architect, Mr. Macgregor Chalmers, to prepare plans.

The restored church

Mr. Chalmers's plans were accepted by the Heritors in November 1913 and approved by the Presbytery of Ayr in February 1914. The estimated cost was £2,000, but expenses rose after the outbreak of World War I. The total expenditure in the end was £2,701/16/0, most of which was paid by the Heritors, the congregation subscribing £727 and the Baird Trust £200.

The restoration was very thorough. It perhaps went a little too far, impairing the 18th century character of the church. New windows in the English style, with small leaded panes, were substituted for the old Scots sash-windows (recently replaced); the original harling of the outer walls, which the Heritors' Records show was whitewashed from time to time with 'Muirkirk lime,' was stripped off (this has also recently been replaced) and the elliptical stone arch over the Bargany loft disappeared.

But four long-standing complaints - stuffiness, darkness, dampness, and lack of seating room - were very practically dealt with. The ceiling was taken out, and as the roof timbers were found to be badly worm-eaten the church received a complete new roof covered with Ballachulish slates. The remaining Heritors' private rooms were abolished and their lofts, which had formerly met at the corners, were set well back. There was thus much more air space.

The south gable was rebuilt and the Bargany aisle was lengthened by 10 feet and lit by a new tall round-headed window facing east. The two other gables were also rebuilt and the old 'fore-stairs' eliminated. Gas lighting was installed. The church got a complete new floor, with asphalt underneath. The old pews, described as 'too high, too narrow, and too straight in the back,' were replaced by new ones of pitch-pine 'of the most modern and comfortable pattern.' A vestry was added adjoining the west gable. Finally, Mr. Chalmers designed a new pulpit and Communion Table, as well as an iron gate to be erected in front of the tower door. The pulpit was set beside a window to give it a better light.

The work was finished in the spring of 1915, when the inside walls (which a hundred years before had been pale blue) were painted 'a light ivory'. In 1920 they were repainted a light grey.

Other improvements and alterations have been made since. They include the insertion of stained glass windows, the installation of electricity in 1947, the restoration of the old external harling, whitewashed as before, and the remodelling of the whole area round the pulpit which itself has been moved back to its central position of 1766. But substantially the church remains as it was reconstructed in 1914-15.

In 1927, soon after the care of the church had passed from the Heritors to the General Trustees of the Church of Scotland, an independent architect, Mr. Alexander Weir, wrote appreciatively of the 'simplicity, fitness and beauty' of the building, adding: 'The belfry tower in particular, which is the dominant feature of the whole composition, is a delightful piece of Renaissance work, which the Dailly people have reason to be proud of'. The tower is also praised as "a charming composition, with rusticated quoins and urn finials" in Mr. George Hay's recent Book *The Architecture of Scottish Post-Reformation Churches.*

Furniture and Ornaments

Prominent in the church today are the stained-glass windows. All of these are modern and most of them inserted since the 1914-15 restoration. Almost the oldest is that in the Bargany loft placed in 1907 in memory of the Countess of Stair (grandmother of Sir Frederick Dalrymple-Hamilton). She lived for many years at Bargany, a kindly old lady much loved in the parish for her charitable works. The gradual addition of other coloured windows has rather unfortunately reduced the extra daylight admitted by the alterations of 1914-15, so that artificial light is almost always needed.

The window which occupies the middle of the south gable was presented by the Woman's Guild in 1921 (the year after the Heritors added the porch to the Bargany door). In 1922 the Turnbull memorial window was inserted to the west of the pulpit, and the Heritors and Kirk Session agreed to the suggestion of Mr. Macgregor Chalmers (who had just died) that if the four north windows were filled with stained glass the designs should be uniform, each with a symbol above and a picture below, and represent, from left to right, the Nativity, Transfiguration, Crucifixion and Resurrection. The Crucifixion was accordingly the subject of the window added to the east of the pulpit in 1927 commemorating Mr. and Mrs. Robert Inglis.

Mr. Inglis had been for many years factor at Bargany and also clerk to the Heritors. He and his wife had presented the two brass flower-vases (1916) and the cross (1919) for the Communion Table in memory of their three sons killed in action during World War I.

The Church's most generous benefactors have been the Todds of Trochraig. They carried on unknowingly an old tradition, for Mr.

Robert Boyd of Trochraig, who died in 1627, left 'twenty pundis to help to by ane bell to the kirk of Daylie'. Mr. and Mrs. George Todd's first gift was the silver baptismal basin in 1919. In 1920 they gave the organ, to replace the harmonium used till that time, and endowed it with a capital sum of £2,000 for its upkeep and an organist's salary. The Kirk Session, in recording their gratitude, observed, 'This noble gift will do much to improve the services of the church to the greater glory of God'.

Mrs. Todd added a brass commemorative plate to the organ in 1929 and also presented a stained-glass window in memory of her husband. In 1947 their children Mr. David and Miss Helen Todd gave, in memory of their parents, the church's present electric lighting system to replace the gas lighting installed in 1914.

The small brass table lectern was, with an alms-dish, a gift from the Reverend and Mrs. George Walker in 1929, soon after Mr. Walker's induction to the charge of Dailly.

To the late Sir North Dalrymple-Hamilton of Bargany we owe the collection plates and their wooden stands (1915). What had happened to the former collection plates is uncertain. The Reverend Charles Goodall had introduced collection bags, an innovation so unpopular that one elder declined to hand them round. In March 1915 the Session resolved to discontinue their use, and the gift of the new plates and stands was made in April.

A very important piece of equipment is the church bell hung in the tower. Its diameter is just under 19 inches. It bears the inscription 'Revd, Dr. C. Cunningham, 1815'. Mr. Cunningham was our minister from 1806 until his death in 1815, and the bell was presumably given in memory of him.

Plate

Our Communion plate is, for so old a congregation, rather undistinguished. We once possessed two silver cups and a flagon which may have been as fine examples of old Scottish craftsmanship as those of

Straiton and Colmonell. They are mentioned in the Session's minutes of 1711 and 1755. But later, being 'old and broken', they were sold.

Our present vessels are comparatively modern, and the large flagon and the six cups are only silver-plated. Four of the cups bear the inscription 'DAILLY - 1833', the other two are uninscribed. Our six platters are of silver, made in 1937. There is also a portable miniature Communion set for taking the Sacrament to sick people. It was made in London in 1914 and presented by Mrs. Robertson Cameron, whose husband, an Army chaplain, had used it in France in World War I.

The old Bible

Our oldest possessions, dating from the time when the church at Old Dailly was still in use, are a number of lead Communion tokens, crudely made and stamped 'DALY', and the ancient pulpit Bible, now used only at the annual 'preaching' at Old Dailly in memory of our Covenant martyrs.

This Bible, printed at Amsterdam in 1679, bears on its title page the initials 'Th. Sk'. These represent Mr. Thomas Skinner, the 'indulged' minister of Dailly from 1665 to 1689. The pages are much worn, especially those of the Psalms. The leather binding has been twice repaired in modern times. This treasured Bible is specifically mentioned in the Session Minutes in 1711, 1755 and 1903.

The Kirkyard

After the removal of our place of worship from Old Dailly the kirkyard there was little used, and for the next 200 years, until the opening of the present cemetery, the parishioners of Dailly were buried around the 'new' church. Many of them acquired their own family 'lairs', and some of the older inscriptions seem more an assertion of property rights than a memorial to the dead: 'This is the burial place of Andrew Crauford, 1754', or, with no date, 'This is the burial place of James Blain and Marion Davidson his spouse and their children'. Two inscriptions of 1722 and

1729 even specify 'four graves breadth'. A lair being heritable property, there was some reason for this precision.

There are nearly 200 memorial stones, but undoubtedly many people were buried in unmarked graves, and a few burials were marked only by rough, unshaped stones with no epitaph.

The oldest inscription is of 1704. There are two of 1716, and several of the years 1720-30. Some of the oldest are best cut. Many stones carry interesting carving, either of simple decoration, of 'emblems of mortality', like a skull or an hour-glass, or of the tools once used by the deceased. One bears a much-weathered coat-of arms, probably that of Alexander Kennedy of Drumellan, who was an elder and the father-in-law of Mr. William Patoun, our minister, and died before 1734. Not all of this carving is professional work. Some of it is crude, and in many inscriptions words are quaintly mis-spelt. But nearly all show care and devotion, and much of the old lettering is beautifully done.

The inscriptions have suffered badly from weathering, and especially from the severe frosts of 1963. But all those decipherable have now been copied, and a full indexed catalogue of them is kept in the vestry to assist enquirers. The names commemorated include many long known in the parish, like Alexander, Currie, Dick, Girvan, Kennedy, McBlain, McCrindle, McIlwraith, McWhinnie, McWhirter, Reucastle, and Scobie; and some old Carrick and Galloway names now grown very rare, such as Drynan, McFedries and McKergow.

Mr. Patrick Crauford, the first minister of Dailly after the Establishment of 1690, was buried at Old Dailly, but in our kirkyard are the graves of his next three successors, Mr. William Steel, Mr. William Patoun, and Mr. Thomas Thomson, The last was the father of Thomas Thomson, Deputy Clerk Register, Scotland's greatest archivist, and John Thomson, the first great Scottish landscape painter, who succeeded his father as minister of Dailly (1800-1805), but was called to Duddingston. These two eminent men, having spent most of their lives elsewhere, have no memorial in their native parish.

Two later ministers are also buried here, Mr. Charles Cunningham and Mr. David Strong. All the ministers' memorials are fairly well preserved except Mr. Patoun's tablet on the south gable which is rapidly crumbling away (though the inscription is recorded).

Here also are buried two outstanding Dailly schoolmasters, Mr. James Scot (1765), who has the only Latin inscription, and Mr. James Welsh (1817) who gave the Thomson brothers their early education. There is, too, Alexander Blair (1862) 'for many years doctor for the parish of Dailly'; But a dead man's trade or calling is not often recorded, though one notices a smith, a wright, a miller, a few merchants, and of course several farmers, one (1737) being 'John Wilson late in Maxwelstoun, an eminent Farmer of severe probity'.

There are many graves of former household or estate servants of the Bargany, Kilkerran and Dalquharran families, commemorated by their employers for long and faithful service.

The most famous inscription in the kirkyard is of course that over the grave, near the south wall, of John Brown, collier, who was entombed for 23 days in the Kilgrammie pit in 1835 and 'quietly expired' three days after his rescue. No other inscription is so informative about the deceased. Most are brief and factual. Occasionally there is a pathetic word or two of mourning, very seldom a text or a moral reflection. But one stone at the main gate, extremely worn, says much in six words: 'This is the burial place of John Stevenson, his Wife and children. Life - how short. Eternity - how long. 1757'.

The Heritors had their family burial 'aisles' at Old Dailly, but all traces of the Kilkerran one there has long vanished: it was disused in the 17th century when the family was non-resident for three generations. Sir John Fergusson, 1st Bt., was buried in 1729 in the ruined castle of Kilkerran. His son, the judge, Lord Kilkerran, was buried in the kirkyard in 1759, when the Session recorded that his son Sir Adam gave 'five pounds sterling to be distribute among the poor of the paroch'. Over his grave, apparently in 1778, Sir Adam built the high stone 'aisle' or vault which stands conspicuously in the middle of the kirkyard. There is record of repairs to its roof in 1804. In it were buried Sir Adam himself in 1813, his successors Sir James and Sir Charles and seven others of the family. There is nothing to be seen inside the building but a memorial stone and two bronze tablets.

The care of the kirkyard has concerned both the Heritors and latterly the Kirk Session for many years. About 1888 when the road on the north side of the church was altered, some gravestones there were removed and set round the church's outside walls. In 1895, 1902 and 1909, as also more recently, some oversized trees growing in the kirkyard were felled, and in 1899 and 1907 'saplings growing on any of the lairs' were ordered to be removed. In 1910 the present north walls and railings, the main gate and pillars, were erected in memory of Dr. Turnbull, our minister for 39 years, the parish contributing £80 and the Heritors the balance of £45. Some of the kirkyard ground was levelled and the Church Officer had orders that the grass 'be cut twice a year at least'. Sir Charles Fergusson 'undertook.to provide some shrubs for planting in the middle of the churchyard' in 1923.

It was typical of the Session's care for this ground in which so much parish history is recorded, that in 1925, when they could have handed it over to the County Council 'it was decided to retain the custody of the village churchyard'.

Changing Ways

The church itself, its furnishings and surroundings, are no more than the setting for our congregational life. That life has continued for many centuries, unbroken but often changing and developing, especially in methods and manners of worship. Our Kirk Session records, which go back to 1692, tell us of many things which we regard as fixed by long tradition but which once were new and sometimes aroused objections which took time to die down.

Arrangements for the Lord's Supper, for instance, were very different in 1766. In those days a long temporary Communion Table used to be set up - a fixed one may still be seen in the church of Carsphairn - round which gathered as many of the congregation as possible. The dispensation was repeated with one relay after another till all present had partaken, three or four other ministers assisting the parish minister.

This ancient practice was abandoned in 1873. On 7th April 'the Session having taken into consideration the plan which has been followed in dispensing the Sacrament of the Lord's Supper, namely by the tables succeeding each other, it was agreed that ... at the Communion to take place on the 7th of May next and at all future Communions, the plan of Simultaneous Communion, which is being so generally introduced throughout the country, be adopted in its stead'.

Five years later, in 1878, it was decided that there should be 'cards of admission to the Lord's Table' instead of the metal tokens which had been distributed until then.

In former times the day appointed for the Sacrament was always preceded by a Fast Day, which included a special service of preparation and was observed like a Sunday, work on a Fast Day being as strictly discouraged as on a Sunday itself. This observance gradually declined until the Fast Day became nothing more than a public holiday. So in 1905 the Session unanimously decided to abolish the Fast Day service, since 'the day has been changed by public use and wont, from the purpose for which it was originally instituted by the Church'. A few parishioners sent a petition to the Session objecting to this decision, but the Session adhered to it.

Services were much longer in the old days than the hour or so to which we have grown accustomed. Only a short interval separated the morning "diet of worship" from the afternoon one which did not become an evening service until artificial light was introduced. The shortness of the interval was the reason why the Heritors had their private rooms behind their lofts. In these the lairds and their families, who had mostly driven some distance to church, rested and ate a light luncheon before returning to their seats for the afternoon service. My great-aunt Mrs. Kennion, who died in 1938 at the age of 99, remembered this as the regular Sunday routine of her childhood.

Praise and prayer

In 1766 and long afterwards the praise at every service consisted simply of psalms and, later, paraphrases, sung unaccompanied under the leadership of the precentor who gave the note with pitch-pipe or tuning-fork. Gradually these were supplemented by hymns. A Dailly Sacred Music Society was founded in 1828 but did not last long. On 3rd November 1873 'the Session unanimously decided that the "Scottish Hymnal" should be used for the first time in the church at the evening service on Sunday first'. The 'Revised Church Hymnary' now in use was adopted in February 1930.

The singing remained unaccompanied till 1877. But on 24th December 1876 Sir James Fergusson, on his being ordained an elder, offered to present the church with a harmonium. The Session took time to consider this offer, but on 22nd January, 'no objection having been discovered', it was accepted. The harmonium continued in use till the presentation of the pipe-organ by Mr. George Todd in 1920.

There has been another very noticeable change in the manner of worship. This is recorded in a minute of 6th November 1882 when the Session discussed 'the desirability of a change of posture at the exercise of praise and prayer during Divine Service'. Till then our congregation, like others, had followed the tradition still observed by the Free Church and by the Lutheran Church in many European countries, standing to pray and sitting to sing. But now 'it was unanimously agreed to ask the congregation to stand at singing and sit or kneel at prayer during Divine Service, and the Moderator was requested to intimate this decision of the Session to the congregation at the commencement of Divine Service on the first Sunday after Communion'.

Nearly all the changes here described took place during the long ministry (1869-1908) of Dr. George Turnbull. He was the last minister of Dailly to have been presented by the Crown before the abolition of patronage in 1874. In his time, also, fell the last occasion when a delinquent was summoned to appear before the Kirk Session for rebuke. This, then, was the period of transition during which our congregation moved, not without due thought and caution, from the old ways into the now established practices of modern times.

The Ministers of Dailly

The Pre-Reformation period

Before the Reformation the priests who ministered in Dailly were appointed by the monks of Crossraguel to which it, like the other parishes of Carrick, was annexed. The names of only two of them are on record:

1516-1537 GEORGE BLAIR, vicar, also officiated as a notary public.
1546 RICHARD ALLASOUN, curate.

Since the Reformation [list updated to 2004]

For several years after the Reformation it was difficult to find ministers for all the parishes in Scotland. Our first two ministers had for a time to care for the people of Girvan and Ballantrae as well as Dailly.

1563-1568 JAMES GREG, translated to Colmonell 1568.
1571-1590 JOHN CUNYNGHAME, translated to Girvan.
1590-1591 ALEXANDER BOYD, deprived for absence from the charge.
1591-1599 DAVID BARCLAY, translated to Maybole.
1605-1640 JAMES INGLIS, threatened with silencing and banishment by the Archbishop of Glasgow for not conforming to the Five Articles of the Perth Assembly.
1641-1659 JAMES INGLIS - no relation to the above.
1660-1663 ANDREW MILLER, deprived by Act of Parliament 1662 but continued to minister until removed.
1665-1689 THOMAS SKINNER, an 'indulged' minister or 'King's curate', but deserted the charge at the Revolution.
1691-1710 PATRICK CRAUFORD.
1711-1723 WILLIAM STEEL.
1724-1755 WILLIAM PATOUN.
1756-1799 THOMAS THOMSON.

1800-1805 JOHN THOMSON, youngest son of the above. Called to Duddingston.

1806-1815 CHARLES CUNNINGHAM.

1816-1840 ALEXANDER HILL, D.D., appointed Professor of Divinity at Glasgow; Moderator of the General Assembly 1845.

1841-1843 WILLIAM CHALMERS, joined the Free Church at the Disruption and was first Free Church minister at Dailly; went to England and became Principal of the English Presbyterian College.

1843-1855 DAVID STRONG.

1855-1869 CORNELIUS GIFFEN, translated to Edinburgh Trinity.

1869-1908 GEORGE TURNBULL, D.D., the last minister presented to the parish; he wrote "A South Ayrshire Parish".

1908-1925 CHARLES GOODALL, son-in-law of the above, translated to Edinburgh St. Oswald's.

1924-1929 DAVID A. DUNCAN, translated to Kilmadock.

1929-1945 GEORGE W. WALKER, remained as minister when the local union of the Parish Church and the former United Free Chureh was effected in 1937.

1945-1949 R. STUART LOUDEN, translated to Edinburgh, Kirk of the Greyfriars.

1949-1956 J. GOLDER McGREGOR, translated to Logiealmond.

1957-1963 DUNCAN S. MacGILLIVRAY, M.B.E., demitted the charge.

1963-1965 WILLIAM D. MACLEAN, demitted the charge.

1966-1968 CHARLES Y. McGLASHAN, C.B.E., D.D.translated to St Andrews Holy Trinity

1969-1975 JOHN STEWART LOCHRIE, demitted the charge

1976 Linked with Barr

1976-1983 RICHARD SMITH, translated to Denny Old.

1984-2000 GEORGE HELON, retired.

2000-   IAN K. McLACHLAN

10

The Plague in Ayr - 1606

In Jacobean Scotland the ravages of 'the pest' were a recurrent feature of life, especially in the burghs. The records of Parliament and Privy Council alike show many acts and orders meant to check its outbreak or spread, for watching the seaports to prevent the landing of infected strangers from abroad, for keeping infected Scots out of this or that town, and for postponing any assembly of the lieges likely to become victims of an epidemic.

Till well on in the 17th century the pest seemed never to die out. It waxed and waned, broke out, raged and sank down here or there, like a smouldering moor fire never quite stamped out. No part of the country or section of society was free from this perpetual and dreaded danger. It was rife in Edinburgh and the adjacent towns in 1597, in Dumfries in 1598, in Findhorn in 1600, in Glasgow and the west country in 1601 and 1602. Not only the poor and the close-packed merchant communities died of it. In 1585 Parliament had had to take notice that 'the pestilent seiknes spreading amongis divers of the greitest baronis' had suspended the meetings of the courts of justice 'and the chancellarie had na established place.' [1] In a serious outbreak the King's court itself might flee from Holyrood, Linlithgow or Dunfermline, and the consequent loss of employment or trade be added to the troubles of the plague-stricken town.

The scourge was generally bubonic plague, though the terms 'the pest' and 'the pestilence' may sometimes indicate some other disease. Contemporary writers do not specify its symptoms: they were too well known. Sufficient for them that it was terrifyingly sudden, contagious, swift in its progress, and almost invariably fatal. Its causes being unknown, outbreaks were generally ascribed to the wrath of God. Neither the physicians nor the administrators of those days had any idea that the carriers of the plague were the rats that not only swarmed in the people's homes, warehouses and barns, and even gnawed the public records, but fattened on the middens of household rubbish, butchers' refuse and fish-guts that lay stinking about the streets and were constantly replenished.

They did however realize that in the filthiest purlieus of their towns the plague seemed to break out first and linger longest and that the presence of garbage - by poisoning the air, perhaps - seemed to assist it. They dimly grasped that cleanliness was some protection. When plague threatened, therefore, orders went forth to clear away the 'middingis' - which accumulated again as soon as the danger passed.

Otherwise, the only remedy was to isolate and immobilize the sick. Ruthlessly, with penalties of branding, banishment, or imprisonment - or even death - the authorities strove to arrest all movement of the infected that might spread the contagion.

The efforts of a municipal authority to cope with an outbreak of the pest can be followed in great detail in the burgh records of Ayr, a town which suffered several visitations in the 16th and 17th centuries but none so destructive as the one of 1606.[2]

As a market town serving a wide district, a seaport enjoying considerable foreign as well as coastwise trade, and the centre of justice of a sheriffdom, Ayr was always receiving incomers who might bring infection with them, and control and inspection of them was vital. In the outbreak of 1597 the town council had strictly enjoined that all entry to the town should be confined to the four 'ports'[3] - the Sea Port at the foot of the Boat Vennel which opened on the quay along the riverside, the Brig Port which guarded the far end of the mediaeval bridge, and the Kyle and Sandgate Ports through which roads led into the country southwards.

Year by year thereafter the town council took their precautions, appointing 'visitors' and 'quartermasters' as health inspectors. In 1603 they resumed a plan to build a hospital, and tried, but unsuccessfully, to persuade a 'chyrurgeane' of Stirling, one John Fergusson, who had family links with Ayrshire, to 'duell within the burgh'. In 1604 they took repeated precautions against the entrance of infected persons, and in 1605 they ordered 'the portis to be keipit in respect of the new infectioun of the pest in Edinburgh, Leyth and utheris eist partis, according to the former actis.'

The neighbouring burgh of Newton-on-Ayr just across the river took similar precautions. In 1603 its council ordered 'the haill toun dykis to be biggit sufficientlie with all diligence for outhalding of all strangers suspect of the pest,' and in 1604 took measures to have goods feared to carry infection taken out of the town. A certain Robert Hamilton, a tailor, had brought possibly infected cloth 'out of Irland,' and one Hew Currie and his partners had been 'intromitting with the Inglis merchantis guidis suspect of the pest.' [4]

Nevertheless the plague broke out with great violence in Ayr and Newton-on-Ayr in July 1606. It cannot have been unexpected. The Ayr council had taken alarm in June and passed yet another sanitary measure, ordering 'the haill middingis and fuilzie' lying about the streets to be removed within 15 days, and none to be deposited in the streets or market-places thereafter for more than 24 hours, under a penalty of 40 shillings for each offence - *'toties quoties.'*

It was on Tuesday, 29th July, that the town clerk for the first time wrote the ominous word 'Pest' in the margin of his minute-book which was to continue to indicate minutes on this subject for the next six months. The council were beginning to isolate the town. No one was to be 'ressavit furth of Cuningham without sufficient testimonial' and none to 'gang to Edinburgh to transport ony geir without the tounis licence,' for it was from the north and east that they feared the plague's attack. But the enemy was within their gates already, and two days later, in a full meeting of the council under Provost David Fergushill, who was in his seventh year of office, they solemnly recognized the awful fact:

'Seeing it hes plesit the almychtie God to vesit this sinfull toun with the seiknes of the pest justlie deservit for the sinnis thairof and contempt of his Word and for the unthankfulnes of the samin towardis his majestie for all his blissing and benefeittis bestowit thairupoun, the provest, baillies, counsale and communitie presentlie convenit, crafing mercie and grace at the handis of our greit God and hevinlie father for our sinnis, throw Jesus Chryst his onlie sone our blissed Saviour and Redemer, and to mitigat his anger and wrath for this pure sinfull toun, for the keiping of the samin ... be the meanes outwardlie, hes nominat and chesit the personis following to be quartermasteris of this burgh during the tyme of the said seiknes.'

Eight men were appointed to supervise each of the four quarters into which the town was divided. They included prominent merchants and tradesmen, the master of work, and John Mure in Carcluy, 'callit the Barroun Mure,' a small landowner.

These quartermasters, bearing batons as a sign of their authority, were to visit their quarters diligently, and all cases of sickness were to be reported to them. All under suspicion of contracting the sickness were to be removed to the Foul Muir and to remain there until the quartermasters sanctioned their return. No one was to 'cum ovir ony bak dykis or ony uther part or port of the toun bot to enter at the portis' only. The penalty for infringing any of these regulations or disobeying the quartermasters was to be death.

The sinisterly named Foul Muir was a stretch of waste ground outside the Kyle Port to the south-east. Here were to be erected wooden huts or 'ludges' under the master of work's supervision or the quartermasters', and in them, or at any rate on the Muir, the sick and the suspect were to remain until they died or were certified fit to return to the town. This rigorous order was accompanied by strict injunctions that the poor wretches must behave themselves properly. There must be 'na hurdome nor filthiness ... nor na blasphemie of Goddis halie name' - and this too 'under the pane of deid.' It is hardly to be supposed that the council seriously meant to inflict the death penalty on a mother who hesitated to take her child to the Foul Muir or an overwrought man for an irrepressible oath; but they had to bring home to the people the vital urgency of the measures they decreed.

On 2 August they appointed two official cleaners, 'for cleynging of the infectit houssis of this burgh.' One was a local man, John Bryane in Crosbie, the other a burgess of Glasgow named James Greynleis who had an assistant ('his boy'). The high wages which the town contracted to pay them - £18 a month to the former and £20 a month to the latter - indicate the danger of the work and the difficulty of finding anyone to undertake it. Bryane was given a month's pay in advance and promised also that 'gif he discharges in his cure ane honest faythfull dewitie toward the toun he sall haif of yeirlie stipend of the toun eftir the clingeing thairof of this pestilence xx *l*. be the yeir for his lyftyme,' and moreover 'to be admittit ane freeman of the toun.'

The cleaners' duties were not limited to the disinfection of houses. They included collecting infected clothing and boiling it in cauldrons. For one such 'kettle' the council paid £28.[5] Fees were fixed for the cleaners besides their agreed stipend, eight shillings for every house cleaned, 6s 8d for each 'kettill or cauldroun full of claithis' and 13s 4d for 'ilk kill full of claithis or uther geir.'[6]

Throughout August the pest advanced and spread. People were afraid to come near their neighbours. The streets became silent and deserted. The country people kept away from the stricken town and the markets were empty. Wrights and masons who had been repairing the quay fled from their work 'be intervening of the pest.' [7] The Kirk Session ceased to meet; and legal business was suspended. For the common ceremony of giving sasine on the transfer of property, parties, witnesses and notaries assembled only twice within the burgh boundaries during August and only once thereafter till the end of the year. On the second of the August occasions, Thursday the 14th, John Batie, a smith and burgess, resigned a property in the Sandgate in favour of his younger son. He fell ill soon afterwards, made his testament on 1 September and died on the 9th.[8] He may have caught the plague in the Sandgate but more probably elsewhere since he was one of the quartermasters.

On 14 August too a merchant burgess of Edinburgh, William Speir, arrived at Ayr with official intimation to the provost and magistrates of the meeting of the Convention of Royal Burghs to be held in Burntisland on the 20th. Probably he did not enter the town but talked to the magistrates from a safe distance at the Brig Port. They sent their excuses for the absence of their representative 'be ressoun of the pestilence quhairwith thai ar veseit at this tyme.' Speir delivered this message to the Convention at their meeting on the 20th and the customary fine for non-attendance was dispensed with. [9]

The visitation of Ayr, said the magistrates' message, was 'notourlie knawin to the haill cuntre', and the Privy Council, sitting in Edinburgh, took notice of it a week later. They must have received a petition from the town council revealing that their ordinances of 31 July had not been respected. There was, according to the Privy Council's record, 'a verie grite mortalitie of all degreis and rankis of personis' in Ayr, and the plague was 'lyke to have a forder course and progres within the said burgh be occasioun thair is na government within the same nor na obedience gevin to the magistratis, bot the suspect and foull personis takis libertie at thair pleasoure to resort amang the clene, some of thame conceilling thair seiknes and the gritest part refuseing to contene thameselffis in sic pairtis and placeis as is appointit to thame for abyding of thair tryell and clengeing.' [10] In other words, people were refusing to remove themselves to the Foul Muir and defying the quartermasters.

The Privy Council granted Ayr special powers to make acts and rules for the government of the burgh, though with no indication of how they were to be enforced, and to make provision for the poor 'quha hes not moyane to mak thair awne interteynment;' and some relief was afforded to the most distressed. Food and coal were ordered at the town's expense. One poor woman, 'suspect of the pest,' received a grant of 16s 8d, and another, Helen Craufurd by name, who took into her house 'twa litill barnes the tyme of the infectioun,' £1 18s 8d. [11] But during the first ravages of the pest the most essential help, skilled medical attention, was lacking. The proposed hospital, though apparently building, [12] was not finished, and there was no resident physician.

By early September, however, a doctor had been engaged, James Harper, and on the 6th Provost Fergushill and Bailie Duncan McAdam made a formal contract with him. He was 'to do his utter and exact diligence ... in curing of ony seik folkis quha hes na moyan of thair awne' at the town's expense, and the council undertook a guarantee of his fees from 'sic as hes moyan of thame selffis.' The Kirk Session on their part engaged to provide him with a special seat in the church 'convenient that he may be fund easilie quhen ony hes adoe with him without truble ather to the minister or heareris of the Word.' [13] Harper evidently took up his duties with energy and won good opinions, for on 20 October the council made him a burgess and guild-brother and promised to pay him £100 as soon as the epidemic was over.

Whatever physical aid could be provided - and it cannot have been much - the people of Ayr had little spiritual consolation at this time, for they had no regular minister. Their minister had been Mr John Welsh, married ten years before to the youngest daughter of John Knox; but, sharing the uncompromising spirit of his father-in-law, he had, with thirteen other ministers of the Church, fallen foul of King James VI and with five of his brethren had been sentenced to banishment for life on the charge of treason. At this time he was in prison, and on 7 November was shipped from Leith to France, never to return to Scotland. He had been only a few years in Ayr, but his powerful preaching had won him such respect that the people still regarded him as their minister even in his banishment and for several years thereafter the town council regularly remitted his stipend to him. The vacant charge was not filled for some months after Mr Welsh's banishment.

There are no statistics of the mortality in Ayr during this dreadful time, but the number of poor folk who died can be guessed from the number of prominent burgesses or their wives whose deaths are recorded. Stephen Harper, a merchant, died on 21 August, and another quartermaster, John Mure, 'the Baron', next day. Before the month ended David White, a cutler, Duncan Craufurd, a mariner, and Jonet Kennedy, another mariner's wife, had died. During September the dead included, besides John Batie the smith, John Boyd, a cordiner, John Farie, another smith, John Cathcart, a rich merchant and shipowner, as well as Bessie Johnstoun his wife, and William Stevin, not a burgess but a man of property. There died also in September the wives of John McCaw, Andrew McAlmont, a merchant, John Gettie, a cooper, and John Smyth, all burgesses of Ayr. Many others died in Newton-on-Ayr, and others in Irvine.

All these were people whose testaments are recorded,[14] and a fact that shows the horror of the time is that, whereas recorded testaments do not normally mention the cause of death, in all these instances it is particularly stated that the testators died 'of the plague of pestilence' or 'of the contagious pest'. Details given bear witness of the rapidity with which death often followed on the first symptoms. Many, having made their testaments verbally, that is naming their heirs and executors before witnesses, it would seem immediately on their seizure, died within twenty-four or forty-eight hours thereafter. Some seem to have collapsed on the ground and immediately sent for executors and witnesses and dictated their testaments where they lay. David White the cutler's testament was made 'be his awin mouth in his awin borne [barn] ... quhair he wes lyand bedfast' in the Cow Vennel (now Alloway Street), and he died the same day. The merchant Stephen Harper made his verbal testament in a neighbour's house and died, perhaps there where the plague had seized him, three days later. Jonet Fergushill, a cooper's wife, died a few hours after making her testament 'at hir duelling hous in Air at the stair fute thairof.' Three other people made their testaments in their 'ludges' on the Foul Muir, and death took them speedily, one, Thomas Liddell, a baker and burgess of Ayr, 'within vij houris thaireftir.'

The most vivid glimpses of such a sudden illness and death appear in the long testament of John Cathcart. He was a man of family, related to the laird of Carleton; he appointed Lord Cathcart 'his chief' and John Cathcart younger of Carleton to be 'oversmen' to his executors, one of whom was the latter's uncle, Allan Cathcart of Clauchfin. The plague clutched him as he was walking by the river outside the town on 10 September, 'besyd the commoun bornes of the said burgh of Air, upone ane grein bra besyde the wattir of Air,' and then and there he sent for John Wallace the notary and dictated his testament as far as he could, empowering another notary, George Angus, to sign it for him 'becaus he was not abill to subscryve the samin him self becaus of the vehemencie of the said diseis quhairwith he was contractit.' Four witnesses were collected, or perhaps had been sharing his last walk: a bailie, two burgesses, and a servant of Lord Cathcart's.

He died two days later. His friends had not, it seems, carried him home, perhaps not daring to touch him, but erected some rough shelter over him on the green brae where he had fallen, for he left money to pay for twenty-four fir planks 'to be ane ludge to the defunct to remaine in.' Anyway, 'the infectioun of the said plague was within his hous and merchand buith.' His wife, Bessie Johnstoun, died of it; his 'compt buik' and other business and private papers were regarded as unsafe to handle, and there was 'laik of clengeris [cleaners] to transpoirt the samin to him for inspectioun thairof.' His executors had other difficulties in making up the inventory, for all his clothes had been carted off to the Foul Muir for the compulsory disinfection.

Cathcart had been a merchant with wide interests; part owner, too, of a ship bought in Danzig which had goods of his on board. He had business in Campveere and imported iron, salt and wine. Oats, bere and wheat lay in his barn and he owned two good horses, one grey and one black. After allowing for his debts, his estate was valued at over £3,000.[15]

It was not only in Ayr, Newton-on-Ayr and Irvine that the plague raged at this time. One death in October specifically ascribed to it was that of Thomas Kennedy, a 'wobster' or weaver, in the parish of Kirkmichael a dozen miles to the south, so that it must have spread into rural Ayrshire as well.

Its continuance was partly due to the resistance of the people to being consigned to a loathsome banishment on the Foul Muir. Where death was so near and so frequent, not even the threat of the death penalty for disobeying the town council's orders had much effect. As early as 6 September the council substituted the lesser but possibly more effective deterrents of branding and imprisonment - 'to be brint with ane hait irn on the cheyk or ony uther part the juges plesis, besyd punisment in the theiffis hoill at the will of the juges, or stokkis'. But the death penalty was inflicted at least once, on Hew Brown, a tailor; and a man and a woman were sentenced to be branded 'for cuming af the Foull Mure' - all on 16 September.

On 7 October another man, Robert Lorimer, was convicted of another offence - 'committing of hurdome upon the Foull Mure of this burgh with Jonet Kessane' - and sentenced 'to be brint upoun the cheyk.' He escaped this penalty, however, on the condition of his becoming the 'lokman' or town executioner. The plague had perhaps killed off the previous holder of this despised office at whose hands, presumably, the unfortunate Hew Brown had suffered. The lokman's salary was five pounds a year. Lorimer was to hold his post for at least twelve months and to serve also as an informer against any misbehaviour on the Foul Muir at an additional stipend of 6s 8d and a peck of meal a week. He accepted this alternative to being branded, and moreover 'frelie grantit' that if he absented himself from his duties he should be 'hangit to the deyth.'

At the Michaelmas burgh election David Fergushill was replaced as provost by Adam Stewart. This does not imply any dissatisfaction with Provost Fergushill's leadership during the epidemic, for he and Stewart alternated in the office - a common way of preserving harmony in a town council - between 1603 and 1608.

The new council's first act was to appoint the lokman. Three days later they agreed on a 'stent and taxatioun' to raise £4,000 from the town to meet the expenses of dealing with the pest and the 'sustentatioun of the pure'. On 20 October they renewed the decree that 'foull personis' leaving the plague camp for the town or bringing into it 'ony foull geir' should be 'brint with ane hait irn on the cheyk or uther placis'.

But the deaths from the pest mentioned in the commissary records are somewhat fewer in October than in September, and by November the scourge seems to have been diminishing. People who had earlier fled from Ayr to escape infection were beginning to return, and the council, on 29 November, ordered them to 'keip thair houssis and nocht to cum furth thairof during the space of ten dayis efter thair hame cuming'. On 29 December, the last Sunday of the year, the Kirk Session met again, considering that 'the Lord's rod was removit'.[16] Early in January the town council too recognized that 'it hes plesit God in his mercie to withdraw his hand af this burgh be deliverance thairof in sum mesour fra this contagious seiknes'. The camp on the Foul Muir was now deserted, the 'ludges' were falling down, and neglected cattle were trying to find a bite of grass among them. It was still thought prudent, however, as late as 24 January, to order suspect persons to keep their houses for fifteen days, and on 10 February to discourage social gatherings for fear lest any lingering infection should spread again - wedding parties were to be limited, on pain of a £10 fine, to 'sex upoun ather syd' and there was to be 'na convocatioun of weymen' at baptisms, or at least only 'sex women at the fardest'.

But James Harper the physician had been paid his promised £100 on 3 February, a sign of the 'quenching and ceissing of the said seiknes'. He remained in Ayr, the council paying the rent for his house, and was still practising there in 1615.[17] On 10 February the council were plainly trying to bring the town back to normal order. 'The haill foull houssis within this burgh' were to be cleaned with all diligence, and the doors to be broken in for that purpose if the owners declined to deliver up their keys. By the early spring the council's main preoccupation was to persuade the townspeople to pay the 'pest stent' to meet the heavy expenses the visitation had cost the community.

What the sum total was of human grief and suffering can hardly be guessed. As already mentioned, most of the deaths of which there is record were of comparatively well-to-do people, That the Dean of Guild's accounts for 1605-6 could not be presented to the council 'be ressoun of his departing this lyf' perhaps indicates that he too perished of the plague. The master of work's were lacking too because of 'his absence afeild the said yeir for the maist part and intervening of the pest'.[18]

There are only glimpses of the deaths of humbler folk, such as 'Roger Rob, cordiner, quha departed of the pest, ane pure man'. [19] The council had to appoint a new drummer on 13 January - his predecessor, in office in July, had perhaps been another victim - and the names of the official cleaners in 1607 are different from those appointed in August 1606,[20] so that Bryane and Greynleis may have succumbed to the daily risks of their work. There were many widows and many orphans for whom executors were settling dead men's estates, and the town's trade, internal and external, must have taken long to recover. The tradition in later years was that the pest of 1606 cost Ayr two thousand lives. [21]

1 Acts of the Parliament of Scotland, ii. p.380.

2 Scottish Record Office, B6/18/1. See also chapter on 'The Plague' by Drs. John Jackson and Jean Dixon in *The Royal Burgh of Ayr*, ed. Annie I. Dunlop (1953).

3 James Paterson: *History of the County of Ayr*, i. p. 162.

4 *Ibid.*, pp. 214-5. The Newton-on-Ayr records quoted by Paterson have since been lost.

5 *Ayr Burgh Accounts*, ed. George S. Pryde (Scottish History Society), p. 232.

6 *Ibid.*

7 *Ibid.*, p. 233

8 Ayr Burgh Register of Sasines; Glasgow Testaments, 1 Sept. 1607.

9 *Records of the Convention of the Royal Burghs of Scotland*, ii. pp. 217-8, 224.

10 *Register of the Privy Council*, 1st series, vii. p. 248.

11 *Ayr Burgh Accounts*, pp. 232, 236.

12 *Ibid.*, pp. 220, 230.

13 Quoted by the Rev. John H. Pagan, *Annals of Ayr in the Olden Time*, p. 66.

14 Glasgow Testaments, vols. iv and v.

15 Glasgow Testaments, iv. ff. 134-5.

16 *The Royal Burgh of Ayr*, p. 277.

17 Glasgow Testaments, xvi. ff: 214-5.

18 *Ayr Burgh Accounts*, p. 229.

19 *Ibid.*

20 *Ibid.*, p. 236.

21 *Statistical Account of Scotland*, i. p. 92.

11

A Wine-Merchant's Letter-Book

In 1950 there was deposited in Her Majesty's Register House the letter-book of a firm of wine-merchants which carried on business in the town of Ayr during the early years of George III. It was in a very tattered and fragile condition and had lost one or two of its opening pages and portions of others; but on being repaired and rebound it could be thoroughly examined, and turned out to be of unusual interest. It covers only four and a half years, from the autumn of 1766 to the early months of 1771; but even in that brief period the business of the firm, Alexander Oliphant and Company, ranged from Stirlingshire to Barcelona, touched many social levels, and dealt with several other commodities besides wine.

The firm was founded in 1766, and the names of the eight partners were recorded some years later in a bond registered in the Books of Council and Session.[1] Four of them, Alexander Oliphant himself, John Christian, George McCree and Robert Whiteside, were merchants in Ayr; the other four were small lairds - Gilbert McAdam of Merkland, Dr. John Campbell of Wellwood, William Logan of Castlemains and David McClure of Shawwood. McCree and Christian shortly became landed proprietors also; for McCree, in 1770, bought Pitcon, in the parish of Dalry, from the last of the Boyds of that name; and Christian, in 1772, bought the little estate of Cunningpark, near the mouth of the Doon, from Captain Hew Whitefoord Dalrymple.[2] By 1774 no less than five of the eight partners were on the roll of parliamentary voters for Ayrshire, who at that time numbered only 128.

The group touches the circles of both Burns and Boswell. David McClure of Shawwood was the man who, as Burns admitted, 'sat for the picture' of the harsh factor in *The Twa Dogs*,[3] and Dr. Campbell was the brother-in-law of John Ranken or Rankine of Adamhill, to whom he wrote one of the most outspoken of his *Epistles*. Dr. Campbell also attended Mrs.

Boswell in her last illness.[4] Boswell knew Gilbert McAdam and many of his near relations.[5] The firm's customers, moreover, included several of Boswell's acquaintance.

Although the beginning of the book has been destroyed by damp it is clear that it began with the firm's inauguration. On 24 October 1766 a correspondent was told, 'We have not yet engaged a wine cooper, and as our cellars are not finish'd and consequently our stock not laid in, we will not have occasion for one for a while'. By early December, however, a cooper had been engaged, and the cellar was built - though actually above ground, and, says one letter, 'on a sand bank'. It was on sloping ground with an easy approach to its entrance from the harbour. It is still in use to-day, and still holds wine.

By the spring of 1767 business was already brisk. Alexander Oliphant and Company seem to have aimed at building up a connexion all over the south-west of Scotland. Before long they also had customers in the north of England, and through an agent in Greenock were exporting wine to the West Indies. But their main business evidently lay between Clyde and Solway. Besides their headquarters at Ayr, they had cellars of their own in Glasgow, Kilmarnock, Moffat and Stranraer. In 1770 they were negotiating for another in Lanark, and also writing detailed instructions to their agents in Greenock, Robert and Alexander Sinclair:

We hope you have got a good cellar to keep the wine in, so that it will be cool in summer and pretty warm in winter. You shou'd have catacombs in the cellar and the wine shou'd be pack'd on the side of the bottles with sarvings of timber.

It was probably due to the social standing of some of the partners that the firm seems to have built up very quickly an extremely promising connexion with many well-known families. Some of their customers were wealthy, and must have entertained on a large scale. One of the first was the Duke of Montrose. In October 1766 his chamberlain was ordering on his behalf two hogsheads of claret; and three years later he ordered three hogsheads. The second consignment was ordered after the firm had sent six bottles of claret 'for a tryal', with the message, 'The wine we propose sending is very old and don't doubt it will please his Grace's taste'. The six bottles were sent by Thomas Hunter, carrier, 'with directions to leave it with the Buchanan carrier at Mr. John Scott's in the new wynd in the Trongate, Glasgow'.

Lord Marchmont was another customer, who, in September 1767, was sent seventy-five dozen of claret and madeira; and William Mure of Caldwell, Baron of Exchequer, was another who liked to order his claret by the hogshead - 'which', wrote Alexander Oliphant, 'we shall be carefull in the choice of, and hope it will please your taste'. Another Baron of Exchequer, John Maule of Inverkeilor, formerly M.P. for Aberdeen burghs; Patrick Craufurd of Auchenames, a former member for Ayrshire; the Earls of Cassillis and Dumfries and Sir Thomas Dunlop of Craigie were other customers who had large accounts with Alexander Oliphant and Company. Sir John Cathcart of Killochan appears once, with an order for a puncheon of rum.

Before the firm had been in existence for more than a few months, the partners decided to build a ship of their own in which to fetch their consignments of wine to Ayr. In April 1767 they placed an order with an Ayr shipbuilder named John Fraser. The ship, a sloop of fifty tons, was built in the course of that summer and launched in October. She cost £600 and was named the *Buck*. It was fortunate that she was ready so soon, for in December the company had news that the *Nelly*, Captain Brackenridge, on which they had apparently been depending hitherto for their cargoes from abroad, had run ashore in the West Indies, during a voyage from Madeira to Ayr by way of New York. She had had fifteen pipes of madeira on board consigned to Alexander Oliphant and Company, and they lost over £700 worth of goods in her and only recovered some £200 through insurance.

The *Buck*, however, which made her maiden voyage to Cadiz and Madeira in the spring of 1768, served her owners well. The skipper, after the first voyage, was one Captain William McRae, and he seems to have been conscientious and skilful. The letter-book contains copies of his sailing orders and also of the orders he carried with him to the company's agents in Madeira, Cadiz, Lisbon, Oporto, Barcelona, Bordeaux and Guernsey, from which a very fair idea can be had of the *Buck*'s cargoes, and occasional glimpses of what sort of passages she had. Sixteen days was reckoned a good passage from Lisbon to Ayr.

The one misfortune the firm suffered through the *Buck*, as far as the letter-book's evidence shows, was the fault of neither the company nor Captain McRae. It happened in the early summer of 1769. The company heard from their agents at Oporto that their ship had been seized by the Portuguese customs authorities, as 'some of the scoundrells of sailors' had been smuggling tobacco on board. The agents managed in a few days to get the ship cleared, but the sailors were detained in prison, and when the news got to Ayr the company seem to have been a good deal embarrassed by the clamour of their relations round the office doors. They wrote to the agents asking if it would be of any use to raise a fund in Ayr for the men's release; but this plan apparently hung fire. The following February a letter repeats, 'The sailors' wives are very uneasy about their husbands'. In March the agents found means at last to get the men out of jail, having apparently advanced the money for their fine - unless perhaps a bribe to the authorities worked equally well. It was not, however, until June that Alexander Oliphant and Company heard about it, and then they wrote,

We wish you could have let us know before the sailors were set at liberty what sum would have been expected as we doubt it will not now be so easily got, however we will try what can be done.

The names of several other ships besides the *Buck* appear in the correspondence, such as the *Peggy*, the *Hercules*, the *Greyhound*, the *Mally* and the *Flora*. The two most picturesque of these names are the *Seaflower* and the *Charming Molly*, a brig from Bristol. One skipper bore a name that might have inspired Stevenson - that of Captain Hannibal Lusk.

The *Flora*, a Greenock brig, came to a sad end in the bay of Ayr on the 8th of December 1770, and her fate is described in one of the longest letters in the book, written by Alexander Oliphant and Company to her owner, Mr. James Gammell.

We are extremely sorry to advise you of your brig Captain Francis's misfortune in being forc'd on shore here this morning in a hard gale of wind at north-west about 10 o'clock and about half-flood. The sea was so high that it was some time before any body could think of going off to her which a few sailors did at last at the risque of their lives in order to save the people on board. They got 3 seamen on shore but the captain, mate and boy refus'd quitting the vessell so that [they] continued from that time till about 4 o'clock in [a ver]y distress'd situation being almost constantly under water till the people on shore ventur'd again off with the boat and brought the captain and boy ashore but the mate was dead, occasion'd by fatigue and the severity of the weather. We are much afraid the brig will be loss'd as we hear she is bulg'd, but are hopeful a good part or all of the cargoe will be sav'd except what may be damag'd by salt water. We shall do what lyes in our power to preserve both ship and cargoe and have employ'd some good hands to get what they can out of her this night as soon as the tide leaves her. We apply'd to the captain for what letters or other papers he might have for you, but he says they are all on board in his chest and must be all wett. As soon as they can be got at he will get them dry'd.

The company proved themselves good friends to the *Flora*'s owner, arranging for a cooper to help in landing and securing the goods, 'also a sergeant's command to watch them and keep off all pilferers'. A fortnight later they offered advice against selling the wreck 'by publick auction', and recommended John Fraser, the builder of the *Buck*, if Mr. Gammell proposed building a new ship to replace the *Flora*, suggesting that in that case Fraser would probably give a price for what remained of her, which was apparently her dismasted hull.

To any historian of the Scottish wine trade Alexander Oliphant and Company's letter-book would certainly be of great value for its evidence of the kind of wines which were in favour in the age of Boswell. As might be expected, claret predominates; and it is interesting to read how such famous names of to-day as St. Julien, Cantenac and Margaux were equally esteemed then. Port and madeira were alike evidently popular. The company ordered thirty pipes of port of the '67 vintage in November 1768. White port, sherry, malaga, canary and various red Spanish and white Portuguese wines also figure among their orders, but burgundy very little, and champagne hardly at all. Nor does there seem to have been any demand for Rhine or Moselle wines, except for that favourite tipple of Boswell's, old hock. The company ordered some old hock in July 1768, through their agent in Guernsey, and two years later sent an order direct to an agent in Hamburg, as follows:

By the recommendation of our friend Mr. Charles Fergusson in London [6] we use the freedom to apply to you for some old hock. He mentions that his house in Madeira propos'd sending a vessell to your place this season and hope this may yet overtake her with you. If so you'l please ship on board of her for our account one hundred doz. of old hock. We beg you'l send it good and address it to the care of Messrs. Fergusson and Murdoch in Madeira.... Mr. Fergusson says they had some from you which was esteem' d very good.

A letter of a month later mentioned that the company hoped to buy the old hock at two shillings a bottle, but were willing to go up to two and sixpence. This was quite a high price, for when the price of port went up to 18s. a dozen the company reckoned it an 'extraordinary rise'. Port, sherry and malaga were all in much the same class as regards price, along with the light Spanish and Portuguese wines, which included 'Packarete, a pleasant sweet wine', 'Methuen, a light red wine', and 'White Carcavella '. The expensive wines were madeira and claret; and the 'very old' claret sold to the Duke of Montrose was charged at £30 a hogshead, 'with bottles, corks and all other charges except carriage', or £31: 10s. inclusive. The company's stock clarets were retailed in bottles at prices ranging from 46s. down to 30s. a dozen. These were high prices, but of course the clarets for which they were charged were all vintage wines. The evidence of the letter-book need not be taken as disproving the well-known assertions of all the English travellers in eighteenth-century Scotland about the goodness and remarkable cheapness of claret in all the Scottish inns. Such wine was evidently of the non-vintage kind, as might be expected.

The company did not deal much in spirits. They wrote to their Bordeaux agent in January 1769, 'We find brandy will not do here' - the reason, presumably, being that smugglers could always undersell them. The Clyde coast from Fairlie to Girvan was notorious for the activity of smugglers. Once at least the company ordered some arrack through their Lisbon agent. In whisky they did not deal at all. At this date it was not drunk in the Lowlands.

But the *Buck* carried a good many other things in her hold

besides wine. The company dabbled, at various times, in importing salt, fruit, grain, meat and silk. 'We do a great deal of business in the corn trade', they wrote in 1770. Occasionally they seem even to have chartered the *Buck* to other firms for short voyages: thus in November 1769 she was carrying a cargo of lead from Creetown to Dublin - it had probably come down on packhorses from the old mines at Wanlockhead. Once they sent the *Buck* out to Lisbon ballasted with coal, 'which', they told their agent, 'please sell and credit us the proceeds'. She seldom returned from abroad without various interesting goods stowed among the wine-barrels. One special order to the Bordeaux agent in December 1769 was for burgundy, champagne, 'the oldest and best claret that can be got', cork-wood, vinegar, olives, oil, silk gloves and mittens, anchovies and 'St. Catherine's prunes'. And in September 1770, when Captain McRae sailed for Cadiz, with orders to load wine, cork-wood - 'as much cork-wood as will stow the cargoe' - lemons, sweet and bitter oranges, and 'raisins of the sun' or sultanas, he carried also with him this curious request to the Cadiz agent:

Please send as much strip'd lutestring as will make a gown for a lusty woman. We suppose Cadiz is a good place for buying silk.

The letter-book naturally contains many orders for the essentials of a wine-merchant's business: cork-wood, bottles, and wax for sealing the corks - red, green, black and yellow. Bottles gave the company a good deal of trouble. They got them first from Glasgow, but their cooper complained that the Glasgow manufacturer made the mouths so large that 'there is no getting corks large enough to stop them'. They next tried a firm in Bristol, from which they ordered 100 gross 'for a tryal', to be sent in the brig the *Charming Molly*; and then three Liverpool firms in turn. None of these manufacturers seems to have been dependable enough to supply bottles of the exact shapes and sizes asked; and Alexander Oliphant and Company had in particular great difficulty in getting their favourite size of bottles - 'long thirteens'. 'What we mean by 13's', they wrote to the Bristol firm, 'is 13 bottles to hold 3 gallons, but those you sent us are all quarts.'

They had other difficulties too. In 1770 there was an appearance in Galloway and Carrick of forged banknotes, the first of which reached the company in a remittance from their agent in Stranraer. Some customers, again, were very slow in paying their accounts. Sir Thomas

Wallace of Craigie at one time owed the company over £70,[7] and Lord Dumfries over £125.

Some other troubles were probably due to the partners' inexperience in the wine trade. Despite constantly telling their agents abroad, 'We must have the best.... We depend on your care in choosing the wine.... We beg you'l send good wine. You must know how material it is to have our wines of equal quality to our neighbours',' they seem to have been several times badly or dishonestly served. Lord Cassillis, Baron Mure, Baron Maule and Patrick Craufurd of Auchenames all complained about the quality of certain clarets supplied to them. Some at least of this wine must have come through the Belfast agent with whom the company had dealt in their early months, and to whom they complained in August 1768 that of the last two consignments from Belfast most of the bottles were 'prick'd' and the rest 'very ill tasted'. To some of their customers Alexander Oliphant and Company apologized, and took the bad wine back; but to Mr. Craufurd of Auchenames they protested,

We are convinc'd that if the wine had been used in time it would have pleas'd well but it is loss'd merely by being too long kept for wine of that body. It was in very good order for drinking when we sent it away.... It was exceeding well lik'd and much in demand.

A month later they took back two dozen of claret from Baron Maule, declaring at the same time, 'It is the only wine ever we took back but what was sold in bottles and seal'd with our own seal, and return'd so'.

But the main cause of the company's ultimate downfall seems to have been simply bad financial management. They had their fingers in too many pies, and from the very beginning seem to have been carrying a large load of debt, increased, perhaps, by the loss of the *Nelly* and the building of the *Buck*. Before the company was two years old it was risking its credit in other ventures. A letter of April 1768 says, 'We are now considerably in advance for the cost of the grain got from Ireland and little money coming in'. A few months later the partners describe themselves as 'disappointed in some sums we thought to receive', and negotiating with Mr. John Bushby in Dumfries for a loan of £3000, 'on the joint security of our whole company'. Early in 1770 they were uneasy about the import duty they were having to pay on French wine, their principal stock-in-trade, and toying with a subterfuge for avoiding it. This is revealed in a letter to their agent in Barcelona:

> Pray is it practicable to import wine into your place from the south of France . . . and if so what duty or other charges on it with you and could that wine be ship'd again with you for Brittain as Spanish wine by this manner to save the extravagant high duty which those kind of French wines will not bear? If this could be done it must be unknown to the captain of the vessell who takes it.... Pray let this be between ourselves....

They were nervous in November 1770 about the risk of sending the *Buck* to Portugal in view of the possibility of 'a rupture' with France, though hoping there would not be 'a warr for some time'. But the mortal wound was received three years later through the failure of Douglas, Heron and Company's bank, which closed its doors, after a spectacular career of less than four years, on 12 August 1773. The bank, like the wine company, was an Ayr venture which had spread its activities over a good deal of the south-west of Scotland; and its collapse involved in its ruin a large number of west country lairds and many small business firms. Alexander Oliphant and Company were only one of 'a variety of enterprising companies, engaged in different kinds of foreign and domestic trade . . . all of them closely connected or linked together' and 'all of them partners of Douglas, Heron and Company'.[8] When the bank failed, Alexander Oliphant and Company could not hope to carry on.

The partners suffered individually. John Christian had to raise money by a bond on his newly acquired estate of Cunningpark, which was sold a few years later at the instance of the bank's creditors. Dr. Campbell of Wellwood was 'stripped of nearly all he possessed' and was obliged to sell his family estate.[9] So was Gilbert McAdam, who on his death in 1788 left many debts and no assets but a gold watch.[10] McClure of Shawwood was in financial difficulties in 1783 when he was pressing Robert Burns's father for the arrears of the rent of Lochlie.[11] None the less, the firm seem to have carried on for a while. In 1774 they were borrowing the sum of £1100 from Archibald Craufurd of Ardmillan.[12] But that seems to have been their last effort, and their affairs were shortly in the hands of trustees for behoof of their creditors, Ardmillan being one of the trustees.[13] They must have given up business soon afterwards, but their stock and goodwill were evidently bought by another wine-merchant, for their premises, like their letter-book, ultimately came into the possession of the later, and still flourishing, firm of winemerchants[14] who presented this record of their predecessors' activities to the Scottish Record Office.

1 Register of Deeds, vol. 238, part i (Durie), f. 497.

2 Paterson's *History of Ayrshire* (1863), iii. 189; i. 142.

3 *Letters of Robert Burns*, ed. Ferguson, i, 107,

4 *Private Papers of James Boswell*, xv, 145-6; xvii, 44, 111, 117, 150-1, 159.

5 *Ibid.*, vii, 122, 132; i, 57-60.

6 Younger brother of Sir Adam Fergusson of Kilkerran, later M.P. for Ayrshire.

7 Register of Deeds, vol. 247 (Durie), f. 810.

8 Paterson, *op. cit.*, i. 38-40.

9 *Ibid.* pp. 142, 612.

10 Glasgow Testaments, vol. 70, fl. 803-4.

11 Hans Hecht, *Robert Burns*, 1936, pp. 46-7.

12 Register of Deeds, vol. 238, part i (Durie), f.497.

13 *Ibid.* vol. 242, part i (Dalrymple), f. 689.

14. Messrs Whigham, Fergusson and Cunningham (in Ayr). "Whighams of Ayr" trades today from the same premises. - AF

12

The Carriage with Yellow Wheels

The question arose when we bought the tractor. It grew more serious with each additional piece of machinery for the tractor to tow. Now, with the arrival of the new Danish binder, it is becoming desperate. What, we ask with growing anxiety, are we to do with the carriage?

The carriage is now pushed into the farthest corner of what the present generation calls the garage but mine still refers to as the coach-house. The coach-house runs the whole breadth of the stable-yard, and in the days when there was only one motor-car in the family there was ample room for that and those of any visitors, as also for the carriage, the waggonette, and the pony-cart. These three veterans, retired after long and venerable service, led a sheltered and peaceful life away at the back of the coach-house, in company with the lawn-mower, a few bicycles, and various odds and ends. The pony cart alone emerged from its seclusion now and then. Like other veterans, it returned to moderate activity during the late war, and resumed its retirement afterwards.

* * *

But now there is more than one car in the family. Moreover, the stable-yard is being turned into a farm-steading. And there is the tractor, and all its company.

Another corner has been found for the pony-cart. The waggonette is standing out in the open. But the carriage is still there for the moment. Even with its shafts folded it occupies a space some ten feet long and six wide, space which is already coveted and may soon be requisitioned. There it stands, partly a reproach, and partly a kind of Ancient Monument.

It still has a kind of mournful dignity, and it was once very handsome: dark blue outside, the upholstery within a somewhat lighter blue, the high wheels a bright yellow picked out with lines of dark green, and a crest on each door and on the back panel. The coachmen who once drove it, the grooms who once devoutly polished it, would shudder to see it now. The upholstery is faded and grimy (I think there was a period when hens roosted inside), two or three of the window glasses are gone, and the panels are streaked with dirt. But it is all complete, even to the two big lamps in their brackets on either side of the driver's seat - and moreover it is roadworthy. Two years ago we lent it to take part in a local pageant.

The carriage belonged to my grandfather, who died in 1907, but when it was built I cannot tell. It is probably late Victorian, but it might be Edwardian. I have few recollections of its being in use. The pony-cart has carried my own children. The waggonette I can recall proceeding slowly up the steep, rough road to the grouse-moor, packed with men, guns and retrievers. But the carriage needed a big strong horse to pull it, which had to be hired when necessity really demanded.

As children, we deplored the rarity of this magnificent vehicle's appearances. My mother once explained to us that it was too heavy for our pony to draw, and that we could not afford to buy a horse. One of us thought this attitude lacking in initiative, and asked "Couldn't we bother a horse from somewhere?"

I do retain, however, one vivid recollection of a time when a horse had been "bothered" to draw the carriage to our railway station across the valley. The family was, I think, migrating to London, and all the nursery trunks made a considerable pile to be packed on the roof of the carriage within the iron rail around its edge. It took so long to load this cargo that the carriage did not leave the front door till the train was actually entering the station a mile away. The anxious station-master, who had been apprised of our departure, saw the lamps of the carriage moving down the drive, and, in the kindly style of those far-off days, detained the train for several minutes while the carriage lumbered across the valley and up the station road. The last five hundred yards were a race between the horse, which by then could proceed at a walk, and the station-master's conscience. I believe we caught the train. What I vividly remember is that the driver jumped off the box and ran beside the horse flogging it up the hill, while we children cheered from the carriage windows.

The carriage is the last of a long line of horse-drawn vehicles - a line of which the beginning, as with most pedigrees, is hidden in the mists of antiquity. I recall my oldest great-aunt, who lived to be 99 and was born on the day of her grandfather's funeral in 1838, speaking of a big two-horsed carriage in which, before the railway came down our valley, the family occasionally journeyed to Ayr, taking two hours to cover the 14 miles. That, however, was not their only means of travel, for my great-grandfather's diary says somewhere, in about 1842, "Lady F. drove out in the britchka, and I accompanied her upon horseback."

In my grandfather's younger days there was an old family coachman named Hugh. When my grand-father was re-elected M.P. for Ayrshire in 1859, Hugh was so loyally drunk by the time the poll was declared that my grandfather was obliged to put him inside the carriage and drive home himself. As the carriage drew up at the front door the family rushed out to learn the result, and were astonished to see inside the figure of Hugh, who was unable to do more than nod his head and repeat over and over again, "M.P. - M.P."

On that occasion Hugh was forgiven; but his weakness recurred, and his disgrace came one night when he was driving the ladies home from a dinner-party. The horses knew the road as well as he, and Hugh's condition might perhaps have passed unnoticed had he not, on reaching our lodge gate, suddenly reined them in and exclaimed in a loud and bewildered voice, "Whatna road's this?"

The relic in the coach-house today cannot be the carriage that poor Hugh drove. Nor, certainly, does it accord with the terms of an estimate my grandfather received from a coachbuilding firm in 1880 "for an elegant and highly finished Dress Posting Barouche, similar to one built for the late Earl of Mayo," with a "commodious hind seat for two servants." But still it is a memento of a picturesque past, and I am loth to treat it with any more disrespect than it at present suffers.

You cannot simply throw away a carriage. Only a barbarian would burn it. I should not care to give it to a film company or a circus. What to do with it is a problem still unresolved. But meanwhile we have got to find room for the binder.

The Covenanter

The barren moor his eyes' last vision
They slew him at this lonely spot,
His knell the echo of the shot,
"There lies one canting rebel the less"
His Requiescat of derision.

Nor, riding onward, dreamed the slayer
How some should, in the friendly dark,
Hollow this grave, this headstone mark
Here on the peewit-haunted slope
With psalm triumphant and with prayer.

But on the hill this murmurous noon
We hold in honour him who fell
For conscience sake; but cannot tell
The grave where lies, forgotten ever,
The nameless murderous dragoon.

Bargany

The Carriage with the Yellow Wheels

Sources

The Valley
first appeared in *Scottish Country* in 1938

The Kilkerran Improvers
first appeared in *Lowland Lairds,* published by Faber & Faber in
1949 and reprinted by The Grimsay Press in 2003

The Queen in Ayrshire
The Last Monks of Crossraguel
Master Robert Cathcart of Pinmore and the Carrick Feud
The Fortunes of William Niven
were first collected in *The White Hind,* published by Faber & Faber
in 1963 and reprinted by The Grimsay Press in 2003

The Weird of Drummochreen
Simple Annals
The Plague in Ayr - 1606
first appeared in *The Man Behind Macbeth,* published by Faber &
Faber in 1969 and reprinted by The Grimsay Press in 2004

Dailly Church
was originally published in 1966 as part of the *Guide to Dailly
Church.*

A Wine-Merchant's Letter-Book
originally appeared in *Essays presented to Sir Lewis Namier,*
(ed. Pares and Taylor) published by Macmillan & Co./St. Martin's
Press, in 1956

The Carriage With Yellow Wheels
originally appeared in *The Glasgow Herald,* 15 September, 1955

Index of Placenames and Surnames

A

Adamhill 173
Ailsa Craig 11, 42, 62, 78
Aird 64, 144
Andrew 40, 48, 52
Ardmillan 62, 63, 82, 83, 181, 182
Ardstinchar 62, 63, 66, 82, 87
Argyll 57, 58, 60
Arkland 30, 40
Arran 61
Atholl 58
Auchalton 100
Auchenames 175, 180
Auchenblain 25, 112
Auchinblain *see Auchenblain*
Auchindrane 82, 83, 87, 91, 92, 94
Auchingairn 24
Auchinleck 32, 51, 64
Auchinsoull. 81
Auchinwin 23
Auchleffin 125
Awles 135
Ayr 5, 10, 11, 15, 16, 23, 26, 47, 49,
   56-61, 63-65, 74, 78-80, 83,
   93-95, 103, 105, 108, 111,
   112, 115, 118, 120, 121, 123,
   125, 129, 130, 143, 146-148,
   161-163, 165-176, 181, 182,
   185
Ayrshire 26, 32, 35, 37, 41, 45-53

B

Baird's Mill 101, 102
Bakewell 40

Balcamie 25
Ballachulish 149
Ballantrae 82, 93, 100, 114, 158
Ballibeg 25
Ballochneill 113
Ballochtoull 117
Balmaclanachan *see Barclanachan*
Baltersan 82
Barcelona 173, 175, 181
Barclanachan 23, 24, 25, 29, 50, 62,
   64
Barclay 64, 85, 158
Bargany 9, 45, 53, 61-64, 66, 72,
   73, 77, 78, 80-83, 85, 87, 88,
   90, 91, 93, 94, 107, 116, 119,
   133, 136, 137, 147-151, 154
Bargeny *see Bargany*
Barnbarroch 78
Barr 17, 100, 119, 159
Batie 165, 167
Beaumont 135
Belfast 180
Bennan 62, 64, 83, 95, 112, 113,
   123, 130
Black 126, 131
Blackbyres 144
Blair 24, 30, 71, 79, 125, 139, 146,
   154
Blairquhan 61, 82, 99, 116, 117, 125
Blane 135
Bonytoun 93
Bordeaux 175, 178, 179
Boswell 8, 23, 36, 37, 49, 51, 52, 64,
   173, 174, 177, 182
Boyd 60, 64, 86, 89, 136, 158, 167

Lightning Source UK Ltd.
Milton Keynes UK
UKOW052152040713

213276UK00001B/61/A